Her Ladyship's
GUIDE TO THE
QUEEN'S ENGLISH

Her Ladyship's
GUIDE TO THE
QUEEN'S ENGLISH

CAROLINE TAGGART

BATSFORD

Acknowledgements
In fond memory of Barry and John, who left this world before *Her Ladyship's Guide...* was finished, but will, I hope, be able to raise a glass to it in the next.

Many thanks to Sarah, Tina, Nicola and Rebecca, who were instrumental in bringing Her Ladyship and me together. Thanks also to the numerous friends who contributed their pet hates and pedantries, especially Linda, who came up with lots of confusables, and Carol, who has surprisingly strong views on fine-toothed combs.

First published in the United Kingdom in 2010 by
National Trust Books
1 Gower Street
London
WC1E 6HD

An imprint of Pavilion Books Group Ltd

ISBN 978 19054 0093 5

A CIP catalogue record for this book is available from the British Library.

18 17 16 15 14
10 9 8 7

Reproduction by Mission Productions, Hong Kong
Printed by Bookwell Ltd, Finland

This book can be ordered direct from the publisher at the website www.pavilionbooks.com, or try your local bookshop. Also available at National Trust shops and shop.nationaltrust.org.uk

Contents

INTRODUCTION

Anyone who has just picked up this book may well be wondering two things: who is Her Ladyship, and what is the Queen's English? (And possibly a third: what qualifies the former to pontificate about the latter?)

To take the second question first, the dictionaries define 'the Queen's English' rather baldly as 'correct standard English speech', but Her Ladyship feels there is more to it than that. Fifty years ago, when the issue of 'U and non-U' (of which there will be more in the next chapter) was considered important, using the 'wrong' word (*serviette* instead of *napkin*, *toilet* instead of *lavatory*) or committing such perceived barbarisms as sounding the *l* in *golf* clearly marked the speaker as 'non-U' – not upper class. Nowadays, in Her Ladyship's view, what distinguishes

> *…what distinguishes the well-spoken Englishman or woman is not so much whether they pronounce* **girl** *as 'gel' or 'gurl' as whether they use language correctly and, crucially, Elegantly.*

the well-spoken Englishman or woman is not so much whether they pronounce *girl* as 'gel' or 'gurl' as whether they use language correctly and, crucially, Elegantly.

As to the first question – 'Who is Her Ladyship?' – she is a person of a certain age and a certain level of education. She is also, undoubtedly, of a certain class, although she claims that this is far less important now than it used to be. She admits to being a snob, but she is more a linguistic snob than a social one. She speaks a language that, for the purposes of this book, is called Elegant English. (It will become apparent that Her Ladyship uses the words *Elegant* and *Inelegant* very frequently; she does not say *posh*, and she begs her readers to follow her example. Let this be the first lesson in Elegant English: *posh* is not an Elegant word and it will not appear again in this book.) She also draws a firm line between the Elegant and the pretentious, and disapproves of the latter as strongly as she disapproves of the vulgar, the ugly and the inaccurate in language.

Her Ladyship is not averse to the use of slang, in its proper place. She uses both email and text messaging, though she cannot bring herself to write *gr8* or *lol*. She accepts wholeheartedly that there is no shame in coming from the north of England and very little in coming from North America or the Antipodes. She believes that speaking clearly, taking particular care with the beginnings and endings of words, is a much more important indicator of education (and therefore of 'class') than struggling to say 'bahth' and 'ahsk' if the long vowels do not come naturally. But she recognises that many native speakers of English, whatever their social and geographic origins, feel uncomfortable with their own language – for the simple reason that they have never been taught its rules. They are aware that they have little formal knowledge of grammar or punctuation and fear that other people are going to despise them if they 'get it wrong'. They use words they do not completely understand in an attempt to appear better educated than they are; and they become agitated about whether to say *lunch* or *dinner* in case they betray what they see as their own humble origins. The purpose of this book is quite simply to allay some of these fears.

Speaking and writing correctly is largely a matter of learning and obeying rules. The commonly used expression *I should of known better*, for example, makes the speaker of Elegant English shudder because of its disregard for the way sentences should be put together (see page 28). Correctness also means thinking about and understanding what one is saying. English is full of words that sound similar, but mean completely different things. *Acetic, ascetic* and *aesthetic*, which happen to be the first in Her Ladyship's list in

7

Chapter 4, provide an excellent example: they sound sufficiently alike to be confusing, but one is related to vinegar, another to an abstemious person or lifestyle, and the third to an appreciation of the arts. Muddling them will produce something that is at best unintelligible, at worst hilarious (but, please note, not hysterical – see page 72). In addition, using words that have precise meanings in an imprecise way – saying *definitive* when one means *definite*, for example – both debases the words and deprives the language of subtlety and shades of meaning.

Elegance is more subjective. Certainly it includes recognising and eschewing the 'non-U' words already mentioned, but it also means choosing words carefully, avoiding cliché and the unthinking use of the myriad of ugly expressions that have slipped into modern English by way of business jargon, the media, American television and the internet. No speaker of Elegant English would ever claim to have a *window of opportunity* in their diary or describe an easy decision as a *no-brainer*.

No speaker of Elegant English would ever claim to have a window of opportunity in their diary or describe an easy decision as a no-brainer.

All that said, *Her Ladyship's Guide to the Queen's English* is intended to be precisely that – a guide. Any living language is subject to constant change, and what makes purists raise a pained eyebrow today may well be standard English tomorrow. To shun innovation – in language as in anything else – is to stagnate. But to those who would like to be more confident in the way they speak or write, and to know that they can be 'correct' when they choose, Her Ladyship offers the rules, guidelines and suggestions in this book.

She would also like to take the opportunity to say that there is no need for anyone to feel intimidated by her – or her views on language. She does not consider herself in any way superior to her readers (without whom, after all, she would have no reason to exist). When she uses the word 'common', she means no disparagement: it is intended as a synonym for 'frequent' rather than for 'vulgar' or 'uncouth'. Oscar Wilde's formidable Lady Bracknell was described as 'a monster without being a myth'. Her Ladyship is quite the reverse: she is a myth without being a monster.

1

U AND NON-U

*To the English – and it does seem to be specifically the English,
rather than any other native speakers of the language – speech
and class have always gone hand in hand.*

In 1912 George Bernard Shaw wrote in the preface to *Pygmalion*
(the play that became *My Fair Lady*): 'It is impossible for an
Englishman to open his mouth without making some other
Englishman hate or despise him.' Some 40 years later, when
Professor Alan S.C. Ross published his famous 'U and non-U:
an essay on sociological linguistics', not much had changed.

Professor Ross maintained that 'it is solely by its language that
the [English] upper class is clearly marked off from the others',
though he went on to qualify this by listing some other minor
characteristics of the upper class: a liking for real tennis and
piquet, 'an aversion to high tea', and that 'when drunk, gentlemen
often become amorous or maudlin or vomit in public, but they
never become truculent'. A dubious distinction, some might say,
but the point is that U people instinctively spoke and behaved in a
certain way and were somewhat contemptuous of those who did
not – or, indeed, of those who tried to do so without being 'to the
manner born'. U people were expensively educated, however
unintelligent they may have been (even the notoriously dim Bertie
Wooster had been to Eton and Oxford), and they had a 'polish',
which they felt the non-U lacked.

The novelist Nancy Mitford, whose own upper-class pedigree
was impeccable, took up the subject in an essay on the English

aristocracy (the two essays, along with several others on the same theme, were published in 1956 under the title *Noblesse Oblige*).
Her Ladyship shudders to imagine what Miss Mitford would have thought of instant messaging and 140-character communications: she disapproved of 'any sign of undue haste' in personal communications, preferring not to use airmail except for business

...even in the 1950s not everyone took the concept of 'U and non-U' seriously.

letters and never employing abbreviations such as *Salop, Herts* and *Glos* when addressing envelopes. Her Ladyship would be the first to admit that times have changed, and even in the 1950s not everyone took the concept of 'U and non-U' seriously. Evelyn Waugh, in an 'open letter' to Nancy Mitford, also published in *Noblesse Oblige*, objected to the fact that a fictional family of her creation had only two children: 'Impotence and sodomy are socially O.K.,' he wrote, 'but birth control is flagrantly middle-class.'

Many of the elements of vocabulary that Professor Ross and Miss Mitford classified as U now seem old-fashioned: to pronounce *real* as two syllables would sound decidedly mannered, unless one were referring to a Spanish football team (an unlikely event in Her Ladyship's circles). Professor Ross remarks on a form of would-be-U pronunciation that was often called *refained*: anyone who has seen the film *Brief Encounter* and recalls the proprietress of the station buffet, played by Joyce Carey, will know exactly what he had in mind. It is an interesting feature of a living, evolving language – and a baffling one for those struggling to use it to best advantage – that some of the U uses Professor Ross described would now fall under that heading: pronouncing *tyre* and *tar* identically, for example, or the adverb *just* to rhyme with *best*. Some of his concerns have also fallen by the wayside because of social or technological changes: the word *wireless* used to be U (*radio* was non-U), but is now merely dated. A year after *Noblesse Oblige* was published, the American poet Ogden Nash pointed out that the Wicked Queen in *Snow White* was 'decidedly non-U': Professor Ross would have had her declaim, 'Looking-glass, looking-glass on the wall', but this is another usage that has drifted into the realm of the pretentious.

However, despite the way language and class distinctions have evolved over the last half-century, a number of the words discussed by Professor Ross and Miss Mitford retain their cachet (or stigma). Her Ladyship here offers a summary of the most significant, and adds a few of her own:

Lunch is the U term for the meal eaten in the middle of the day. *Dinner* is eaten at night, or by dogs; *tea* is a drink taken at any time of day, or accompanied by scones, cake and the like in mid-afternoon. (Her Ladyship, by the way, pronounces *scone* to rhyme with *gone*; rhyming it with *bone* leans towards the *refained*.) A light meal in the evening is *supper*, while *luncheon*, although U, was considered old-fashioned even in the time of

When issuing invitations, one should ask people for **dinner** *or* **drinks** *(not to a dinner party or a drinks party).*

Professor Ross. When issuing invitations, one should ask people for *dinner* or *drinks* (not to a dinner party or a drinks party). *Cocktails*, once the U word for such 'mixed' drinks as a gin and tonic, now refers to colourful concoctions containing tequila and pineapple juice. The U term for a gin and tonic is *a gin and tonic*. The abbreviation 'G & T' is non-U.

Vegetables are U; *greens* are not.

Pudding is U; *dessert, sweet* and (heaven forbid) *afters* are not. On the other hand, the old-fashioned insistence on *ices* rather than *ice creams* now sounds affected. *Dessert* is in fact a different course from pudding: it may consist of fruit and/or cheese, but not trifle, crème brûlée or apple tart.

Coffee should normally be used without an article, to refer to the beans or granules from which the drink is made. The drink itself is *a cup of coffee.* To invite someone in for 'a coffee' is decidedly non-U.

Napkin or **table napkin** is U; *serviette* is not. Professor Ross describes this as 'perhaps the best known of all the linguistic class-indicators'.

Living room or **drawing room** is U. *Lounges* are found only in hotels or airports.

Sofa is U; *couches* are confined to the offices of psychoanalysts.

Bike or **bicycle** is U; *cycle* is not.

Ill is U. *Sick* means that the sufferer was actually vomiting.

Lavatory and therefore **lavatory paper** are U; *toilet* and *toilet paper* are not. **Loo** also belongs to polite vocabulary. In anyone over the age of four, discussion of what one does in this part of the house is entirely unacceptable.

Pardon is non-U, whether it is used as an apology for hiccuping or for bumping into someone in passing, or to indicate that one has not heard what was said. *Sorry, I'm very sorry* or *Excuse me* are all better in the first instance; in the second, *What did you say?*, although somewhat abrupt, is nevertheless to be preferred to *Pardon?* A sincere apology, however, may be expressed as *I* do *beg your pardon* and in the sense of *a legal pardon* the word is, of course, perfectly acceptable. On the other hand, *Pardon my French* as a coy apology for the use of strong language is much more Inelegant than strong language itself. Hiccuping, by the way, is not connected with coughing, so the spelling *hiccoughing* is misguided.

Wealthy is considered the non-U equivalent of the U *rich*. Her Ladyship would add as a footnote that, whatever the socio-linguistic merits of the two words, nobody with any Elegance of mind would use either term if it involved speculating on the financial status of an acquaintance.

In one instance modern usage would now say that Miss Mitford was wrong: she insisted on referring to people and things from Scotland as *Scotch*. Nowadays *Scotch* is usually an alcoholic drink, although *whisky* is the more U term; *Scotch* is used largely on licensed premises to distinguish it from Irish, bourbon or any other similar spirit that might be on offer. *Eggs* and *mist* may also be *Scotch;* almost anything else from north of the border (including a person) is *Scottish* or *Scots*.

Le mot juste

It has become almost fashionable among public bodies in Britain to ban the use of foreign words and expressions, a move which Her Ladyship opposes with every fibre of her being. While she is all in favour of the Plain English Campaign's aversion to what it calls gobbledygook, she believes that any language should be able to draw on the rich resources it has garnered across the centuries, whatever their origins.

> *Her Ladyship believes that any language should be able to draw on the rich resources it has garnered across the centuries, whatever their origins.*

In addition to the Latin terms that are embedded in legal language (*habeas corpus*), the French and Italian ones in the culinary world (*cordon bleu, al dente*) and more Italian in music (*allegro, crescendo*), here are some foreign terms that may take their place with pride in the Elegant vocabulary:

apropos (French, the stress is on the last syllable and the s is not pronounced): 'with reference to'. One frequently hears *Apropos (of) nothing at all* as a precursor to a change of subject

ad hoc (Latin): literally 'towards this', but used to mean 'for the moment, for this purpose' as in *an **ad hoc** decision*, a decision that will suffice until there is time to make a more considered one

aficionado (Spanish): a fan or, to use the French equivalent, a devotee. Often used in connection with the arts: one is more likely to be an *aficionado* of the works of Schubert than of a football team

aide-mémoire (French, 'aid-mem-war', to rhyme with 'car' rather than 'war'): a memory aid, such as notes for a speech

bête noire (French, 'bet nwar', again to rhyme with 'car'): literally 'black beast', something or someone that one particularly dislikes. The expression *safe haven*, for example, is a *bête noire* of Her Ladyship's

bona fide (Latin, pronounced as four syllables: 'bone-a fie-day'): 'in good faith', usually used as an adjective to mean 'genuine', as in *His certificate showed that he was a **bona fide** graduate of the Royal College*

carte blanche (French): literally 'white card', used to mean 'absolute freedom', as in *I gave her **carte blanche** over the party, so she invited everyone she knew*

crème de la crème (French; *crème* is pronounced to rhyme with 'them'): 'cream of the cream', the very top rank or level of ability, whether of society or of secretaries

de rigueur (French, 'de reeg-err'): literally 'of rigour', used to mean 'essential, expected', often of evening dress or polite behaviour

de trop (French; the *p* is not pronounced): literally 'of too much', often used of a third person in a room where the other two would prefer to be alone

déjà vu (French, 'day-zha voo'): 'already seen'. *A sense of déjà vu* may be an eerie feeling that one has experienced something before, or a sensation of boredom for the same reason

en route (French, 'on root'): 'on the way', as in *We are driving to York, but we are stopping to visit friends in Nottingham en route*

fait accompli (French, 'fate a-come-plee'): a 'done deed', as in *I knew she would be worried if I told her what I was going to do, so I just did it and presented her with a fait accompli*

faute de mieux (French, approximately 'foat d'myeu'): 'for want of anything better', as in *Charlie didn't invite me to the ball, so I went with Richard faute de mieux*

faux pas (French, 'foe pa'): a false step, usually an embarrassing one, as in *Asking Anna about Freddie was a faux pas – I didn't know they had split up*

femme fatale (French, 'fam fatt-al'): literally 'fatal woman', an attractive woman who seduces men for reasons that may be connected with money or status but are unlikely to have anything to do with love

force majeure (French, 'force ma-zherr'): 'a greater force', as in *I knew she wouldn't stop arguing until I agreed, so I surrendered to force majeure*

idée fixe (French, 'ee-day feex'): 'fixed idea', an obsession

je ne sais quoi (French, approximately 'zhe n'say qwa'): literally 'I don't know what', used approvingly to describe an indefinable quality – often *a certain je ne sais quoi*

joie de vivre (French, approximately 'zhwa d'veev-rr'): 'joy of life', but much more expressive of boundless enthusiasm than the rather tame English translation

laissez-faire (French, 'less-eh fair'): literally 'let do', used in the sense of allowing others to do what they want to do, without interference, as in *a laissez-faire attitude or policy*

mot juste (French, 'mo zhoost'): not just 'the right word' but '*exactly* the right word'. Like *joie de vivre*, this is a much more exciting expression than its literal translation

nom de plume (French): 'pen name', a term used only of writers; other people seeking to disguise their identity use a *pseudonym*, which is Greek in origin; criminals use an *alias*, which is Latin

non sequitur (Latin): literally 'it doesn't follow', used as a noun to mean an illogical remark or deduction

nous (Greek, 'nowse' or 'noose'): 'common sense', as in *Anyone with any nous could have worked out what to do*

nouveau riche (French, 'noo-vo reesh'): 'new rich', used particularly of those who display their wealth Inelegantly

par excellence (French, the last syllable pronounced to rhyme with 'nonce', not 'pence'): literally 'through excellence', used to mean 'the definitive', as in *He is the show-jumper par excellence: I have never seen anyone ride more gracefully*

per se (Latin, 'per say'): 'in itself', as in *I don't object to floral wallpaper per se, I just wonder if it will look right in the study*

pièce de résistance (French, 'pee-ess d'ray-zist-onse'): literally 'piece of resistance', metaphorically 'the outstanding item of a creative artist's work'. The creative artist is often a chef: *All his cakes are marvellous, but the one he made for Helen's wedding was a **pièce de résistance***

pied-à-terre (French, 'pee-eh-da-tare'): literally 'foot on the ground', used of a small dwelling occupied only occasionally, as in *She spends most of her time in the country but she has a **pied-à-terre** in Chelsea*

raison d'être (French, 'ray-zon det-rr'): 'reason for being'. *Helping people to speak more Elegantly is Her Ladyship's **raison d'être***

rapport (French, 'rap-or'): 'a sympathetic relationship', as in *They met only last week but already there is a real **rapport** between them*

RSVP (French): short for *répondez s'il vous plaît*. This is seen on invitations and means 'please reply'. It is a strong argument against abandoning foreign expressions: one's invitees would surely be baffled to read 'PR by 4 September'

savoir-faire (French, 'sav-war fair', with 'war' rhyming with 'car'): literally 'to know how to do', this is used – again with approval – to describe an ability to deal suavely with the day-to-day running of life, for example, *I enjoy going out with him; he has real **savoir-faire** and always seems to be able to find a taxi when it's raining*

sine qua non (Latin, 'see-nay qua known'): literally 'without which not', in other words a condition without which something will not happen, as in *A knowledge of Greek is a **sine qua non** of studying classical architecture*

status quo (Latin): literally 'the condition in which', meaning 'the existing state of affairs', as in *Although I disagree with him, I am not going to argue and risk upsetting the **status quo***

tête-à-tête (French, 'tet-a-tet'): literally 'head to head', used for 'involving only two people', as in *they dined **tête-à-tête** at Romano's*

tour de force (French): literally 'turn of strength', a brilliant or masterly achievement or performance, as in *His portrayal of Othello was a **tour de force***

vice versa (Latin): 'the other way around', as in *We could go to the theatre and then have dinner, or **vice versa***

volte-face (French, 'vault-fass'): 'an about turn, a complete change of opinion or policy', as in *Father had always disliked Victoria's boyfriends, but he did a **volte-face** when she met Toby*

Schools and colleges

The upper classes have always chosen to send their sons (and latterly their daughters) to one of a select list of schools. Many of these have long traditions (Winchester was founded in 1382, Eton in 1440) and the vocabularies specific to each institution are ingrained in anyone connected with them. It would be a major social solecism, for example, to refer to a former pupil of Charterhouse as an 'Old Charterhousian' or of St Paul's as a 'Paulite'. The following list does not claim to be exhaustive, but it covers many of the more prominent schools in England and Scotland.

School	Name for former pupils
Benenden School	Benenden Seniors
Charterhouse (not 'Charterhouse School')	Old Carthusians
Cheltenham College (co-educational)	Old Cheltonians
Cheltenham Ladies' College	former pupils belong to Guild (not The Guild)
Christ's Hospital (also known as the Bluecoat School, Housey and CH)	Old Blues
Dulwich College	Old Alleynians
Eton College	Old Etonians
Fettes College	Old Fettesians
The Godolphin and Latymer School	Old Dolphins
Gordonstoun (not 'Gordonstoun School')	Old Gordonstounians or OGs
Harrow School	Old Harrovians
Marlborough College	Old Marlburians
Merchant Taylors' School	Old Merchant Taylors
Oundle School	Old Oundelians (OOs)
Roedean School	Old Roedeanians
Rugby School	Old Rugbeians
St Paul's Girls' School	Old Paulinas
St Paul's School (boys)	Old Paulines
Sherborne School	Old Shirburnians
Shrewsbury School	Old Salopians
Stowe School	Old Stoics
Wellington School	Old Wellingtonians
Westminster School	Old Westminsters
Winchester College	Old Wykehamists (from the name of its founder, William of Wykeham)

Oxford and Cambridge colleges

The names of some Oxford and Cambridge colleges present challenges to the uninitiated, and, as with the schools listed on the previous page, it is important to get the smallest details right. By the way, no student or graduate of either Oxford or Cambridge uses the word *Oxbridge*: one always feels an affinity to one institution or the other and would not dream of treating the two collectively.

This list does not include all the colleges; only those at risk of being misspelt, punctuated incorrectly or mispronounced. Note particularly the different spellings of Magdalen, Oxford, and Magdalene, Cambridge, though both are pronounced 'maud-lin'. Note too the difference between Queen's and Queens', and between St Catherine's and St Catharine's. In addition, both universities have a Corpus Christi College and a St John's College, spelt alike and, in the latter case, both pronounced 'St John' rather than 'Sinjun'.

> *No student or graduate of either Oxford or Cambridge uses the word* Oxbridge.

Even when the official name contains the word *college*, it should not be used in conversation: *I was at King's, I applied to Balliol*, are the accepted forms. Similarly, if one were invited to a stately home, one would never use the words 'Hall' or 'House' in referring to it. *I'm going to Chatsworth* could imply that one was a guest of the Duke of Devonshire; *I'm going to Chatsworth House* certainly indicates that one will be paying an entrance fee.

Oxford

All Souls College
  (no apostrophe)
Christ Church
  (two words, not 'Christ
  Church College')
Lady Margaret Hall
  (not 'Margaret's')
Magdalen College
The Queen's College
  (named after one queen:
  Philippa, wife of Edward III)
St Anne's College
St Antony's College
St Benet's Hall
St Catherine's College
St Cross College
St Edmund Hall
St Hilda's College
St Hugh's College
St John's College
St Peter's College
St Stephen's House

Cambridge

Christ's College
Gonville & Caius College
  ('Caius' is pronounced 'keys')
King's College
Magdalene College
Peterhouse
  (not 'Peterhouse College')
Queens' College
  (named after two queens:
  Margaret, wife of Henry VI, and
  Elizabeth, wife of Edward IV)
St Catharine's College
St Edmund's College
St John's College

2

GRAMMAR:
HOW ENGLISH WORKS

A book of this kind cannot hope to cover this vast subject in any depth. This chapter contents itself with outlining some of the key elements and considering a few common errors.

Parts of speech

This is the term used to explain a word's function in a sentence. Parts of speech are also frequently described as 'building blocks' – the basic elements from which a sentence is composed. In English there are eight of them: *determiner, noun, pronoun, adjective, verb, adverb, preposition* and *conjunction*. Words can also be used as *interjections;* strictly speaking these are not a part of speech, because they are not connected grammatically to the rest of a sentence, but it is still useful to understand their purpose.

Determiners

The most common of these are the most common words in the language: the *indefinite article (a, an)* and the *definite article (the):*

> *A lord (or **an** earl) was dining at the Ritz* could refer to any, unidentified lord or earl
>
> ***The** lord ordered steak tartare* refers to a specific lord whose identity has already been established

It used to be considered correct to say *an hotel, an historical novel,* probably because upper-class speakers knew that the words derived from French and pronounced them accordingly (that is, without sounding the *h*). In modern English the *h* in 'hotel' and 'historical' is clearly pronounced, so to use *an* is both incorrect and pretentious. The rule is simple: if the following word begins with a vowel (*a, e, i, o, u*) or a silent *h* (see box on page 26), use *an*; if it begins with an audible consonant, whether it is *h, b, c* or any other letter of the alphabet, use *a*.

The exception to this rule occurs when the first syllable of a word beginning with *u* is pronounced *you*, in which case use *a:*

a unicorn	but	*an umbrella*
a unique opportunity		*an underground train*
a usual suspect		*an unpopular decision*

Other determiners define still further which noun is under discussion: **that** *gown* as opposed to **this** *gown,* **her** *jewellery* as opposed to **my** *jewellery,* **half** *the county* as opposed to **all** *the county.*

It is Inelegant to use *this* when what is meant is *a. I saw* **this** *man coming along the road* is right only if it is clear who the man is – *this* man as opposed to *that* one; otherwise the correct form is *I saw* **a** *man coming along the road* (and I am about to tell you about him).

Another common Inelegancy is 'my friend': *I went to the theatre with my friend* implies (sadly) that the speaker has only one friend. *I went with a friend* is what is meant.

Some silent *h*'s

Remarkably few common words in English begin with a silent *h*:

Heir, heiress
Honest, honesty
Honour, honourable etc
Hour

In addition, there are some words of French origin which English still pronounces in the French way, with an 'unaspirated' *h*, which should be preceded by *an:*

Hommage, with the stress on the second syllable (this is usually confined to self-important or satirical conversation about the cinema; the English *homage,* with the stress on the first syllable, has an aspirated *h).*

Hors d'oeuvres

Habitué presents speakers with a choice: English speakers who know French tend to pronounce it as if it were a French word, without sounding the *h,* and this would be Her Ladyship's preference. But the *h* is always pronounced in *habit, habitual, habitation* etc.

To drop the *h* in *herb* is to declare openly that one has lost the battle against Americanisms (see page 90).

Nouns

These are 'naming words' and they are subdivided according to the different things they name.

Common nouns name a person, animal, place, thing or abstract idea, such as *jockey, estate, book, success, happiness*. They can be further divided into *concrete nouns* (anything that can be identified with one or more of the five senses – *jockey, estate, book*) and abstract nouns (which have no physical existence – *success, happiness*).

Proper nouns always start with a capital letter and are used to name a specific person, animal, place or thing: *the Duke of Westminster, Black Beauty, Hampshire, the Louvre.*

Collective nouns are used to name a group or collection of individuals: *an orchestra, a jury, a string of racehorses*. See Agreement, page 36, for more about dealing with these.

Pronouns

These replace nouns, as in *she* or *her* for *Her Ladyship, he* or *him* for *the butler*. See page 34 for when to use *she* and when to use *her*.

Verbs

These are the 'action words' that indicate what is happening in a sentence: *I arrive, you leave, he stays, we entertain, they enjoy*. The basic form of any verb is the *infinitive*, which always begins with *to: to arrive, to leave, to stay* etc. But the infinitive does not describe a complete action: this requires a *finite verb*, which is created either by altering its ending – he *stays* but *you stay, they stayed* – and/or by adding an *auxiliary* or 'helping' verb: *I **shall** stay, you **were** staying, she **might have*** *stayed. Finite verbs* are therefore able to convey whether an action happened in the past, present or future, whether it is continuous or often repeated, or whether it may never happen at all.

> *I **go** to Italy in the winter* (meaning I go every year)
> *I **shall go** to Italy in the winter* (I shall go once, at a fixed point in the future)
> *I **went** to Italy in the winter* (I went once, at a fixed time in the past)
> *I **have gone** to Italy in the winter* (at some point in the past, possibly more than once)
> *I **might have gone** to Italy in the winter* (but I chose to go to Spain instead)

This way of conveying time is called a *tense. Compound tenses* use an auxiliary verb and a form of the main verb called a *participle.* This may be the *present participle* (ending in *-ing*) or the *past participle* (usually ending in *-ed,* but see the note on irregular verbs on page 39).

   When looking at auxiliary verbs, notice how often some form of the verb 'to have' occurs. Consider:

> *I **should have** known better* (but I didn't, so I did something foolish)
> *He **may have** been at Ascot* (but I am not going to tell you whether he was or not)
> *They **could have** afforded that Bentley* (but they chose to buy the Volkswagen)

Not understanding this construction is the cause of what her Ladyship considers one of the gravest errors of all.

   In speech, the above examples are frequently shortened to *I should've, He may've* and *They could've,* with the apostrophe indicating that the *ha* of *have* is missing (see The Apostrophe, page 44). These abbreviations can easily be misheard as *should of, may of, could of.* But *of* is a preposition (see page 31), used to convey connection or possession: *the sampling of a fine wine, the estate of my late father,* and has nothing to do with auxiliary verbs. It should never, ever be used in this context.

Adjectives and adverbs

These are 'describing words', the difference between them being that adjectives describe nouns, whereas adverbs describe verbs, adjectives or other adverbs. Adverbs are often – but by no means always – formed by adding *-ly* to the adjective:

> *She is a **graceful** woman* (adjective, describing the noun *woman*)
> *She sat **gracefully*** (adverb, describing the verb *sat*)
> *I was **extremely** impressed* (adverb, describing the adjective *impressed*)
> *She charmed everyone **very** easily* (adverb, describing the adverb *easily*)

One important subset of adverbs and adjectives consists of *comparatives* and *superlatives,* which are used when more than one person, thing or action is being considered. A *comparative* compares two things; a *superlative* three or more. Comparatives of short adjectives are usually formed by adding *-er* (with a word that ends in *-y,* the *y* should be changed to *i* first):

> *The Eiffel Tower is **taller** than the Leaning Tower of Pisa*
> *Blood is **thicker** than water*
> *Jane is **prettier** than Elizabeth*

With longer words, the comparative is formed by adding *more* or *less*:

> *Jane is **more beautiful** than Elizabeth*
> *Marianne is **less thoughtful** than Elinor*

Superlatives either end in *-est* or are formed by using *most* or *least*.

> *Lydia is the **youngest** of the family and also the **least prudent***
> *Mary is the **most studious***

These examples all use adjectives, but the same applies with adverbs:

> *Emma dressed **more elegantly** than Harriet*
> *Anne spoke **less impetuously** than Louisa*
> *Elizabeth lived the **most happily***
> *Catherine behaved the **least sensibly***

Exceptions to this rule are the adjectives *good* and *bad* (and their related adverbs *well* and *badly*). The comparative of *good* or *well* is *better*, the superlative is *best*. With *bad(ly)*, the comparative and superlative are *worse* and *worst*. A superlative may stand alone: a person may be simply *the best violinist* or a train service *the worst in England*. But a comparative should always indicate the thing to which it is being compared: the signs on public transport urging one to give up one's seat

> *A superlative may stand alone: a person may be simply the best violinist or a train service the worst in England.*

to *someone less able to stand,* while commendable in sentiment, are Inelegant in their form of expression: *someone less able to stand **than you are*** would be more pleasing and take up very little extra space.

A frequent mistake in this area is the use of a made-up comparative, *worser.* This is not a word in modern English. Almost as common – and equally wrong – is adding *more, most, less* or *least* to something that is already a comparative or superlative – *least worst, more handsomer*. English does not duplicate effort in this way: saying the same thing twice should be done deliberately and for emphasis, or not at all.

Remember, too, that superlatives are used with reference to three or more things. *The reddest half of the apple* is therefore wrong, as there can be no more than two halves, one of which may be *redder* than the other.

Prepositions

Prepositions indicate where one thing is in relation to another: *to, by, around, up, behind, near* and so on:

> *The brooch rolled **under** the table*
> *The Labrador ran **towards** the tree*
> *The gardener carried the secateurs **in** his pocket*
> *The librarian removed the book **from** the shelf*

See Too much of a good thing, page 86, for cautions against the overuse of these apparently inoffensive little words.

Conjunctions

These are used to link two or more words or groups of words:

> *Pride **and** Prejudice*
> *Rome **or** Venice*
> *Jack of all trades **but** master of none*
> *I should be delighted to come to your reception, **although** my husband has a prior engagement*
> *My chauffeur is away, **so** I shall have to drive myself*

Interjections

These stand on their own, can often be followed by an exclamation mark and are used to show emotion – sorrow, surprise, fear, annoyance: *Oh no!, Good heavens!, Help!*

Double duty

It is possible for the same word to perform a number of different functions in different sentences and therefore serve as more than one part of speech, depending on the context:

> *It's dark in here – please switch on the **light*** (noun)
> *Her smile **lights** up a room* (verb)
> *I need something **light** to read on the cruise* (adjective, describing 'something')
> *She was wearing a **light** blue gown* (adverb, describing 'blue')

Sentence structure

Parts of speech explain the function of individual words and types of word. The next step is to put them together, which means understanding how a sentence works.

A sentence can be defined as 'a sequence of words capable of standing alone to make an assertion, ask a question or give a command'. It usually consists of 'a subject and a predicate containing a finite verb'.

Sentences can be very simple:

> *The door is opening.*
> *Is that you, Stephen?*
> *You're early.*
> *Do come in!*

or complex:

> *When I saw the door opening I assumed that Stephen had arrived,*
> *although it was earlier than his usual time, and I called to him to*
> *come in.*

A complex sentence may consist of one or more main statements and various subsidiary elements, but the principle is the same.

Subject/object/predicate

The *subject* of a sentence performs the action of the verb; the *object* receives or suffers the action. A simple English sentence follows the pattern *subject, verb, object*:

The train left the station
Sarah loves raspberries
Walls have ears

The subjects are *the train, Sarah* and *walls;* they perform the action of the verb (*left, loves, have*). The objects are *the station, raspberries* and *ears.* The *verb* and the *object* combine to form the *predicate*. So, in the first example, the predicate is *left the station* (finite verb *left* + object *the station*).

Word order may be altered:

- to ask a question: *Has the train left the station?*
  - part of the verb (*has*) precedes the subject (*the train*)
- for emphasis: *Raspberries I love; strawberries I don't care for*
  - *raspberries* and *strawberries* are the objects of the verbs *love* and *care for*

In English (unlike in Latin or German, for example) the form of the noun is the same whether it is the subject or the object:

The station needs repainting
Raspberries are good for you
His ears stick out

In the first group of examples (page 33) *the station, raspberries* and *ears* are the object; in the second (above) they are the subject, but the words themselves are exactly the same.

This is not true of pronouns. Grammatically speaking, pronouns and verbs are divided into the first, second or third person. The first person is the speaker (*I, we*), the second is the person (or people) addressed (*you*), the third is anyone else (*he, she, it, they*). But these are all the subject (or nominative) case; pronouns also have an object (or accusative) case. As objects:

I becomes *me*
You remains *you*
He, she or *it* becomes *him, her* or *it*
We becomes *us*
They becomes *them*

So, for example,

I admired my teacher
My teacher inspired *me*

He loves cricket
Cricket amuses *him*

She bought a new pair of shoes
The shoes didn't fit *her*

We are going for a drive
Why don't you come with *us*?

They gave a lot of parties
Many people visited *them*

This sometimes causes confusion when a sentence contains what is called a *compound subject* or *compound object,* but the same law of subject and object applies:

Tony and I *are going to Barbados*
Gerald is coming with **Tony and me**

There is a simple rule here: a preposition is always followed by an object pronoun. If in doubt, imagine these sentences without the *Tony and. Me are* (or *am) going to Barbados* and *Gerald is coming with I* are clearly wrong; therefore *Tony and me are going to Barbados* and *Gerald is coming with Tony and I* are wrong too.

In constructions such as this, by the way, it is courteous as well as correct to put the noun before the pronoun: *Tony and I* rather than *I and Tony.*

The subject/object applies equally to third-person pronouns: *Her and James dance well together* is wrong. It should be *She and James dance well together,* but *I enjoy watching James and her.* (Remember that the pronoun *you* is both the subject and object form of the second person, so it does not cause the same concerns.)

A similar error creeps into the use of possessive pronouns (see page 40) when more than one person is involved. *I was delighted to hear about yours and Sarah's engagement* may be intended as a friendly remark, but the use of *yours* is ungrammatical. As with the compound subject example above, take out *and Sarah's* and the resulting *I was delighted to hear about yours engagement* highlights the mistake.

Agreement

The subject of a sentence must agree with the verb. A singular noun takes a singular verb; a plural noun takes a plural verb. It really is as straightforward as that.

With regular verbs, the present tense changes only in the third person singular, when an *s* is added to the basic word. The past tense is the same whatever the person. So, to use a regular verb:

> *I dance*
> *You dance*
> *He, she* or *it dances*
> *We dance*
> *They dance*

In the past tense:

> *I danced*
> *You danced*
> *He, she or it danced*
> *We danced*
> *They danced*

With some verbs the third person singular requires slightly more change than the addition of an *s* – *have* becomes *has*, for example, *go* becomes *goes* (and, extraordinarily, in the past tense becomes *went*) and *marry* becomes *marries* – but the real exception to the rule is the verb *to be*. Its present tense is:

> *I am*   *We are*
> *You are*   *They are*
> *He, she* or *it is*

The past is:

I was	*We were*
You were	*They were*
He, she or *it was*	

Whatever the verb, however, the rule bears repeating: the subject (*I, you, we, the Duke of York and his daughters*) must agree with it. Under no circumstances is it acceptable to say *We was*. One's role model is the Queen, not a commercial-radio disc jockey or celebrity chef. Nor indeed the

> **Under no circumstances is it acceptable to say We was.**

BBC Television News, one of whose announcers recently (and shamingly) announced that *nearly all the UK's 250 species of bees is in decline.*

Confusion often arises over *collective nouns* – nouns used to describe a group of people or things. However, the rule is simple: *a herd of cows* may contain any number of animals but there is only one *herd*, so it takes a singular verb.

> **The cows were** *startled by the noise of the tractor,* but
> **The herd of cows was** *grazing in the paddock*

Similarly, *the army, the jury, the orchestra, the House of Lords* are all singular. Many people nowadays feel that strict adherence to this rule is pompous and are uncomfortable saying *the jury is considering its verdict* or *the House of Lords is likely to propose changes to the bill.* Anyone who suffers from such misgivings could avoid the dilemma by adding a phrase such as 'the members of': with *the members of the jury are considering their verdict* or *the members of the House of Lords are likely to propose changes* there is no doubt that subject and verb are both plural.

The expression 'there is no doubt' raises another important point. *There* used at the beginning of a sentence can be either singular or plural, depending on what follows. *There is no doubt* is correct, because *no doubt* is singular; *there is twenty people coming to dinner* is not. The subject of this sentence is *twenty people* and they *are* coming to dinner.

Splitting infinitives

Some two and a half centuries ago, when the rules of English were being laid down by scholars who were well versed in Latin and Greek, it was decreed that it was wrong to split an infinitive – that is, to put any word or words between the *to* and the verb itself. Thus *to happily potter about in the garden* was frowned upon; *to potter about happily* or *happily to potter about* was preferred. In the twenty-first century, iconoclasts are inclined to point out that infinitives in Latin and ancient Greek consisted of one word rather than two, so there was no question of splitting them, and therefore the rule, designed to make English follow a classical model, has always been nonsensical. Her Ladyship believes that clarity and Elegance are far more important than eighteenth-century edicts and that to scrupulously avoid splitting an infinitive and thereby produce a clumsy sentence is to take pedantry too far. In the previous sentence, she is aware that she could have said *scrupulously to avoid* or *to avoid scrupulously*, but she chose not to.

> *Her Ladyship believes that clarity and Elegance are far more important than eighteenth-century edicts.*

A note on irregular verbs

In the majority of cases, the past tense and the past participle look the same: *I looked, I had looked.* But there are exceptions:

> *I wrote* but *I had written*
> *I broke* but *I had broken*
> *I ate* but *I had eaten*
> *I did* but *I had done*
> *I went* but *I had gone*

Her Ladyship begs readers never to use the past participle when the past tense is required:

> *I **done** enough work*
> *I **gone** home at six o'clock*
> *The clock **was broke***

are to be deplored. The correct versions are:

> *I **did** (or **had done**) enough work*
> *I **went** home at six o'clock*
> *The clock **was broken***

Verbal nouns

Verbal nouns or gerunds look like present participles (that is, they end in *-ing*) but they perform the same task as nouns. In the sentence *I am dancing, dancing* is the present participle: it combines with *am* to form a finite verb (see page 27). On the other hand, in the sentence *I love dancing, dancing* is a verbal noun, the object of the verb *love*. Grammatically, it performs the same function as if one had said *I love Paris* or *I love you*.

This matters when a verbal noun comes into contact with a possessive pronoun. Trying to analyse the sentence *He told his grandchildren about him fighting in the war,* one finds that there is no grammatical relationship between *him* and *fighting in the war*. That is because *fighting* is a verbal noun and the word preceding it should be a possessive pronoun. Replace *fighting* with something that is more obviously a noun and this becomes clear:

> *He told his grandchildren about **his** accident*
> *He told his grandchildren about **his** fighting in the war*

Accident and *fighting in the war* are the same part of speech and should be treated accordingly. Similarly:

> *Father didn't want to hear about **my** (not *me*) having missed the bus*
> *I am very envious of **your** (not *you*) going to Nepal*
> ***Our** (not *us*) paying Archie's debts only encouraged **his** (not *him*) gambling*

Greek and Latin plurals

A number of English nouns have been borrowed directly from Greek or Latin and retain their original form; this means that the plural follows Greek or Latin rules rather than English ones.

Unless one has had a classical education to teach one these rules, such words simply have to be learnt.

Phenomenon and *criterion* come from Greek; the plurals are *phenomena* and *criteria.*

Appendix, crisis and *thesis* come from Latin; the plurals are *appendices, crises* and *theses,* with the last syllable pronounced 'ease'. Purists such as Her Ladyship maintain that the plural of *index* is *indices,* but *indexes* is gaining ground.

A number of words ending in *-us* or *-os* which have their origins in Greek or Latin are now regularly treated as 'English' words and pluralised by the addition of *-es:*

abacus	*abacuses* (or *abaci* – the Latin form)
hippopotamus	*hippopotamuses*
octopus	*octopuses*
rhinoceros	*rhinoceroses*
syllabus	*syllabuses*
terminus	*terminuses* (or *termini*)

Four very common English nouns – *bacteria, data, media* and *trivia* – are, perhaps surprisingly, plurals; their singular ends in *-um.* Again, purists insist on a plural verb with these nouns. However, many people now feel that *the data are contaminated* and *trivia about celebrities are filling our newspapers* sound affected, so treating these nouns as singular is becoming acceptable in non-technical language. Referring to *bits of data* or *pieces of trivia* comfortably and accurately skirts the issue.

    Agenda is potentially confusing, as it originally meant 'things to be done' and was therefore plural, but is now widely accepted as 'a list of things to be done' and treated as singular. As with the examples in the previous paragraph, saying *items on the agenda* avoids the problem. Despite its similarity of appearance, *propaganda* reached English through a slightly different route and is (and has always been) singular.

Abbreviations and contractions

Although few people other than grammarians now make this distinction, an *abbreviation* is a shortened form of a word or words in which the ending is missing – *exam* for *examination*, *gym* for *gymnasium*, *DVD* for *digital video disc*, etc. – whereas a *contraction* contains the beginning and end of a word but not all the middle – as in *Dr* for *Doctor*. Sticklers for formality put a full stop after an abbreviation but not after a contraction, though to put a full stop after *exam.* or *gym.*, when the short forms are so widely accepted as words in their own right, would be to stickle indeed. Dictionaries still print *adj.* for adjective and *adv.* for adverb, but in less formal contexts full stops are generally used only for clarity: to distinguish *no.* meaning *number* from *no* meaning *not yes*, for example; or *a.m.* meaning *in the morning* from *am*, a part of the verb *to be*. The Latin abbreviations *etc.*, *e.g.* and *i.e.* (meaning respectively *and so on*, *for example* and *that is*) are other examples where the full stop is commonly used.

When pluralising abbreviations such as *DVD*, there is no need for an apostrophe unless possession is being indicated:

> *I keep the DVDs in a special box*
> > but
> *A DVD's shelf life is lengthened if it is kept free of dust*
> > or
> *All the DVDs' covers were brightly coloured*

No, no, no, no, no

The 'double negative' is the supreme example of duplication through lack of understanding. In English (though not in some other languages, including French and Spanish) two negatives cancel each other out and produce a positive. Used incorrectly, they are among the clearest indicators of Inelegance.

I didn't do anything is correct. The *n't* is short for *not* (see The Apostrophe, page 44), which is all the negation that is required.

I didn't do nothing adds a second negative (*nothing*) and is correct only in a context such as *'I didn't do nothing,' she said indignantly. 'I weeded the garden, baked a cake and took the dog for a walk.'* In this instance the double negative *I didn't do nothing* adds up to a positive *I certainly did do something.* Whichever meaning is intended, pronouncing *nothing* so that it comes out as the slovenly *nuffin* is one of the worst of solecisms.

Other comparable errors include *I looked but I couldn't find him nowhere, I didn't talk to no-one* and so on.

Punctuation

Punctuation marks are used to clarify meaning. A full stop, for example, means that the end of a sentence has been reached – what has just been said is complete; the speaker or reader may pause for breath. A comma indicates a less complete idea and a shorter pause; semi-colons and colons fit somewhere in between.

Old-style rules of punctuation are often ridiculed, but they are there for a purpose: consider how the meaning of the sentence *The butler stood at the top of the stairs and called the guests' names* would change if the apostrophe were omitted.

The apostrophe

This is the most commonly misunderstood and abused of all forms of punctuation, yet the rules for its use are reassuringly straightforward. An apostrophe generally indicates one of two things:

- the absence of a letter or letters
- possession

Absence of letters

This is most common in speech or in informal writing, when abbreviations such as *don't, can't* and *won't* are perfectly acceptable. In these instances the apostrophe indicates that an *o* is missing from the word *not*: the words are shortened forms of *do not, cannot* and *will not*.

Many common words that were originally abbreviations of longer words but are now considered legitimate in their shorter form were once written with apostrophes: *'phone* for *telephone, 'flu* (or, strictly speaking, *'flu'*) for *influenza, 'bus* for *omnibus, 'plane* for *aeroplane*, but this is now considered at best archaic, at worst pretentiously pedantic.

Note, however, that in such cases the punctuation mark at the start of the word is an apostrophe ('), not an opening inverted comma ('). This also applies to abbreviations such as *'Tis* (for *it is*) and – a particular *bête noire* of Her Ladyship's – *rock 'n' roll.* It is not that she objects to the music; she merely deplores the fact that so many people write *rock 'n' roll,* apparently oblivious of the fact that the apostrophes at either end of the word denote the missing *a* and *d* in *and.*

Possession

To indicate that something belongs to someone or something, add an apostrophe followed by an *s* to the name of the owner:

Winston Churchill's speeches
The Queen's birthday
The symphony's slow movement

If the 'possession' belongs to a plural noun ending in *s*, add an apostrophe after the *s*:

The princes' friends (meaning the friends of more than one prince)
The flowers' petals (more than one flower)

If a word is a plural that does not already end in *s*, add *'s:*

The women's conversation
The geese's enclosure

With short names ending in *s* or *es*, add *'s.*

Miss Jones's class
Thomas's doubts

To make a name that already ends in *s* plural, add *es*, and to indicate possession put an apostrophe after that:

> *Mr Evans's dog* but *The Evanses' party*
> *Mrs Prentiss's opinion* but *The Prentisses' conversation*

With longer names, particularly biblical or classical ones, adding *'s* may make the word difficult to pronounce. If so, just add an apostrophe – *St Barnabas' church, Euripides' plays* – or rephrase: *the church of St Barnabas, the plays of Euripides.*

Arguments rage over whether to use *Jesus'* or *Jesus's* when referring, for example, to Jesus's miracles. Her Ladyship believes that euphony – making a pleasant sound – is the deciding factor here: most people pronounce the word 'Jesuses', which is not remotely awkward and makes *Jesus's* a perfectly acceptable possessive. On the other hand, *Hades's* is clumsy and *Hades'* is therefore to be preferred. Again, rephrasing as *the miracles of Jesus* or *the jaws of Hades* avoids any possibility of error.

Note that possessive pronouns: – *hers, its, ours, yours, theirs* – do not require an apostrophe:

> *That book is not **yours**, it is **hers***
> *The blue car is **ours**, the red one is **theirs***

Be particularly careful with *its*, because *it's* does exist – it is short for *it is*:

> *The chihuahua dropped **its** bone on the carpet*
> *I worry about tripping over the chihuahua because **it's** so small*

The shopper's apostrophe

Many prominent British department stores are, to say the least, idiosyncratic in their use of apostrophes, but to make a mistake here is to confess to being unfamiliar with their carrier bags or delivery vans. The correct forms are:

Harrods
Harvey Nichols
Heal's
John Lewis
Marks and Spencer
Selfridges

To refer to Harvey Nichols as 'Harvey Nick's', by the way, is the lowest form of name-dropping, on a par with suggesting that one is on first-name terms with 'David and Victoria' or (if one belongs to an older generation) 'Dick and Liz'.

Hyphens

These little lines used to link parts of a word or phrase are second only to the apostrophe as the victims of abuse or neglect in the world of punctuation. American spelling has abandoned them in words such as *pre-eminent, re-entry, co-operate* and *co-ordinate*, and British English is beginning to follow suit, but Her Ladyship feels they have a place here in clarifying both pronunciation and meaning. In words such as *pre-date* (to come before, as opposed to *predate*, to behave like a predator); *re-cover* (to cover again, as opposed to *recover*, to get better) and *re-prove* (to prove again, rather than *reprove*, to scold), they become essential.

The Americans having invented the concept of *coeducational schools*, they are, Her Ladyship concedes, entitled to spell the word as they choose, but she would still prefer *co-educational*.

Increasingly, hyphens are also omitted in phrases where their inclusion would remove ambiguity, and this is a battle that Her Ladyship will fight to the death. Consider the two possible meanings of *The hotel has a fine dining room*. Does the hotel have a dining room of particular architectural merit, or does it have a room in which fine dining takes place (and perhaps another in which meals of less gastronomic appeal are served)? The humble hyphen allows one to distinguish between a *fine dining-room* and a *fine-dining room*.

Similarly, in the common phrase *the deep blue sea*, what is it that is deep – the water itself, or the shade of blue? *The deep, blue sea* makes it clear that the former meaning is intended, *the deep-blue sea* the latter.

Note that it is incorrect to hyphenate a compound adjective in which the first word ends in *-ly*: *a finely tuned piano, a lightly boiled egg* and *a colourfully decorated ballroom* are all completely unambiguous.

See also the discussion of *a fine-tooth(ed) comb* on page 69.

Some common mistakes

This section deals with a few frequently encountered errors not mentioned above.

That or which?

Many subordinate clauses are introduced with the words *that* or *which*, and the function of the clause determines which is correct. The important distinction is that restrictive or defining clauses give *essential* information; non-restrictive or non-defining clauses give *additional* information. Consider these examples:

> *The Rolls-Royce which was parked outside the front door was a gleaming silver*
> *The Rolls-Royce, which was parked outside the front door, was a gleaming silver*

In the first sentence, the clause *which was parked outside the front door* is restrictive or defining: it 'defines' the Rolls-Royce and is it crucial to the sentence as a whole. Which Rolls-Royce? one might ask. Answer: the one which was parked outside the front door.

In such constructions, the word *which* may be replaced by *that* without loss of accuracy or Elegance. The same is true of:

> *The jacket **which** (or **that**) I bought last week looks shabby already*
> *The poem **which** (or **that**) he read moved me to tears*

If the clause refers to people, *who* should be used for the subject of the defining clause, *whom* for the object:

> *The professor **who** was due to give the lecture arrived an hour late*
> *The students **whom** he eventually addressed were bored*

In speech or casual writing *who* is still required if the noun is the subject of the defining clause (*The professor who was going to give the lecture*), but if the noun is the object *whom, which* or *that* may be omitted altogether:

> *The jacket I bought last week*
> *The poem he read*
> *The students the professor addressed*

See also *The Morecambe and Wise relative pronoun*, page 55.

In the second example – *The Rolls-Royce, which was parked outside the front door, was a gleaming silver* – the words which are enclosed by commas are non-restrictive or non-defining. The important point is that the Rolls-Royce was silver; the fact that it was parked outside the front door is an additional, 'by the way' piece of information. Clauses such as this must always be introduced by the relative pronouns *who, whom, whose* or *which*, not by *that*:

> *Even Helen,* **who** *is the most easy-going of women, was upset by that remark*
> *Vanessa,* **whom** *I have never liked, was particularly unpleasant yesterday*
> *Leslie,* **whose** *dress sense is impeccable, looked elegant*
> *The robin,* **which** *always landed on my balcony at breakfast time, was a cheerful sight*

Note how the use of commas changes the meaning of the Rolls-Royce examples. In Elegant English careful use of such apparently insignificant elements produces a wealth of subtle distinctions that are lost in slovenly speech and writing. Note also that in such cases, commas always go in pairs, like brackets: *The Rolls-Royce, which was parked outside the front door was a gleaming silver* is wrong.

Can/may

Often confused, *can* refers to possibility or ability, *may* to permission.

> *Can I ask you something?* is a foolish question, because you *have* just asked me something, so obviously you *can* (that is, you are able to).
>
> *May I ask you something?* is both polite and sensible, because it means *Is this a convenient moment for you to listen to me?*

Similarly *Can I bring a partner to the ball?* (Do I know a suitable young man who will not recoil at the invitation?) is not the same as *May I bring a partner?* (Do I have your permission to do so?).

The same distinction applies to *could* and *would*. Many people would say *Could I ask you something?* because they think it sounds politer than *Can I ... ?*, but *could,* like *can,* refers to possibility or ability. **Could** *you pick up my dress from the dry cleaner while you are in town?* is asking whether the person has the ability – do they have the strength to carry the dress, or will it fit comfortably on the back seat of the car? *Would you ... ?* means *Would you be willing to ...,* which is the real meaning of the question.

Try to remember...

*I shall try **and** be there on time* is incorrect. Ask the question, 'I shall try what?' Answer: '*To* be there on time'. *And* is meaningless here.

Fewer/less

Some nouns are *countable;* some are *non-countable* or *mass* nouns. A countable noun refers – self-evidently – to things one can count. There may be three people in the room, twenty books on the shelf,

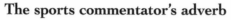

The sports commentator's adverb

As explained on page 29, adverbs are words used to describe verbs, adjectives or other adverbs and are often formed by adding *-ly* to the adjective:

> *The teacher was cross*
> *She spoke to me **crossly*** (i.e. in a cross way)

> *He was a heavy man*
> *He moved **heavily*** (i.e. in a heavy way)

In recent years, however, many sports commentators have chosen to ignore this distinction and say such things as *Federer is serving beautiful* or *Woods drove his tee shot perfect*. In fact, this usage has become so common that it may almost be considered the norm. But only if one is a sports commentator. For anyone else, it is ungrammatical and unacceptable.

An exception to the 'add -ly' rule is *leisurely*, which is both an adjective and an adverb. This means that both *He walked **leisurely** around the park* and *He walked around the park **at a leisurely pace*** are correct, though Her Ladyship considers the latter more Elegant and therefore preferable.

a million grains of sand on a stretch of beach. Mass nouns are things that cannot be counted: there may be a million *grains* of sand, but there cannot be a million sands. With sand, one has an amount, a quantity – a little, a lot – but not a number.

Fewer applies to countable nouns; *less* to non-countable nouns. So if there were three people in the room and one went away, there would be *fewer* people left. If one had a bag of sugar and poured some of it into the sugar bowl, there would be *less* sugar in the bag.

A countable noun refers – self-evidently – to things one can count.

The supermarket cliché *Five items or **less*** is incorrect because one can count those items, so the right word is *fewer*.

Either/or and both/and

The position of these words can alter the meaning of a sentence, as well as displaying Elegance or a lack of it. In both pairings (and in the negative version *neither/nor*), each word of the pair should precede the same part of speech or same construction. Consider these examples:

You can either go to university or find a job is correct: *go to university* and *find a job* are both phrases qualifying what 'you' can do. If one omits the words *either go to university or* one is left with *You can find a job,* which is grammatically correct and makes perfect sense.

You can either go to university or finishing school is wrong, because *go to university* and *finishing school* are grammatically different things. Omit the words enclosed by *either* and *or* and the result is *You can finishing school,* which is grammatically incorrect and meaningless.

Moving *either* so that it is just before a noun produces the correct *You can go to either university or finishing school.* Alternatively, add another *to*: *You can go either to university or to finishing school.* This latter version is preferable because it has the bonus of avoiding a possible ambiguity: *You can go to either university* might be interpreted as offering a choice between Oxford and Cambridge.

Similarly, *She was both disappointed by the weather and the fact that Louis wasn't there* is wrong: the positioning of *both* suggests that two people were involved. All three of the following are correct:

*She was disappointed by **both** the weather and the fact that Louis wasn't there* (*both* now refers to *the weather* and *the fact*)

*She was disappointed **both** by the weather and **by** the fact that Louis wasn't there* (note the insertion of the second *by*, so that the two things by which she was disappointed take the same form – *by the weather* and *by the fact*)

*She was **both** disappointed by the weather and **upset** (by the fact) that Louis wasn't there* (*by the fact* is grammatically correct but unnecessary: *she was upset that …* is complete in itself)

Only

Like *either/or*, *only* should be positioned carefully and as closely as possible to the word it qualifies. One hears, all too frequently, sentences such as:

*We **only** drank two glasses of champagne*
*They **only** went on holiday in September*

In the first instance, 'we' are suggesting that we might perhaps have *eaten* another glass of champagne, or poured another glass over someone's head. That is clearly not what is meant: the word the speaker means to qualify is *two*. *We drank **only two** glasses of champagne* emphasises that 'we' did not drink three, four or 17.

*They **only** went on holiday in September* says that 'they' did
nothing else but go on holiday during the entire month of
September – they did no work, visited no friends, read no books.
Again, this is obviously not what is meant. The correct version is
*They went on holiday **only** **in September*** – meaning that they did not
go in August or October.

The Morecambe and Wise
relative pronoun

Ernie Wise's 'play what I wrote' and Glenda Jackson's
'beauty like what I have got' delighted a generation that
had, by and large, studied grammar and knew that these
were deliberate illiteracies for humorous effect. For the
benefit of younger readers, *what* should be used as a
pronoun only in indirect questions such as *Do you have any
idea what you are doing?* (a sentence in which the direct
question *What are you doing?* is implied).

In the first Morecambe and Wise example, the correct
wording is *the play **that** I wrote*. In informal contexts, *that* may
be used also to refer to people: *the woman **that** I met on the
train;* in formal contexts *the woman **whom** [object] I met on the
train* or *the woman **who** [subject] was on the train* is preferable.

The second example managed to pack three
Inelegancies, not to mention a vulgar boast, into six words
– no mean feat! *Beauty such as mine* is probably the most
Elegant way of saying what is meant; *beauty like mine* would
be acceptable in informal speech; *beauty such as I have* is
correct but sounds rather affected. See also *like*, page 76.

The estate agent's pronoun

Increasingly heard, and not only from estate agents, are
sentences such as:

> *I'm sure this property will be exactly what yourselves are
> looking for*
> *I'd be delighted to show it to yourselves*
> *The deal was negotiated by my colleague and myself*

These are all examples of the misuse of emphatic pronouns.

> *I'm sure this property will be exactly what **you** are looking for*
> *I'd be delighted to show it to **you***
> *The deal was negotiated by my colleague and **me***

say the same thing far more Elegantly. In none of these
instances is there any need to stress the pronoun, so the
use of the emphatic form trivialises it and, over time, will
make it less effective in its original sense. *Myself, yourself* etc.
should be reserved for sentences such as:

> ***Myself**, I should prefer not to live on such a busy road* (although
> I acknowledge that it is convenient for you)
> *You should negotiate the deal **yourself*** (rather than
> persuading someone else to do it)
> *He was determined to prepare his presentation **himself*** (with
> no help from anyone else)

Her Ladyship also begs her readers not to be frightened of
the word *me*. As explained on page 34, it is simply the
object pronoun corresponding to *I* and is perfectly correct
when following a verb or a pronoun. As she might say
herself, 'Do, please, listen to me.'

The television presenter's demonstrative pronoun

A commonly heard tautology is *these ones* or *those ones*. *These examples, these specimens, these objects* would be perfectly correct, because the nouns (*examples, specimens, objects*) convey additional meaning. *These ones*, on the other hand, says nothing more than *these*. The reason Her Ladyship attributes the blame for this phenomenon to television presenters is that she once heard the host of a gardening programme, checking how her seedlings were faring, refer to *these two ones here*. A lesser person than Her Ladyship might have screamed.

It should go without saying that a demonstrative pronoun should agree (in terms of whether it is singular or plural) with the noun that it qualifies. Yet educated television presenters have also been heard to say *these kind of films*, when either ***this kind*** *of film* (any number of films of a certain kind, such as romantic comedies) or, less probably, ***these kinds*** *of film* (any number of films of more than one kind, such as romantic comedies and thrillers) is correct.

Misrelated participles

These are sometimes known as dangling modifiers, but Her Ladyship prefers to avoid expressions that might provoke unseemly mirth. In the sentence *Driving through Tuscany, Thomas was charmed by the sight of so many hillside villages,* the words *driving through Tuscany* form what is known as a participial phrase, *driving* being the present participle of the verb *to drive* (see page 28). Although the subject of the phrase is not expressed, it is understood: Thomas was doing the driving. The sentence is grammatically correct and its meaning is unambiguous, because – to put it technically – the subject of the participial phrase is the same as the subject of the main clause and the participial phrase is positioned as closely as possible to the noun it modifies. *Driving through Tuscany, the sight of so many hillside villages charmed Thomas* or *Thomas was charmed by the sight of so many hillside villages driving through Tuscany* are both inaccurate and potentially comical: neither the sight nor the villages are likely to have been at the steering wheel.

Consider also: *As a dedicated supporter of this theatre we are very pleased to be able to make this offer to you for a preview of our new play.*

Grammatically, this says that 'we' are a dedicated supporter, whereas clearly the meaning is that 'you' are the supporter. Rephrasing the sentence to begin *As you are a dedicated supporter of this theatre, we are pleased* ... or *We are pleased to make this offer to you, a dedicated supporter of this theatre* ... would have taken only a little thought and effort, and produced something flawless.

3

A MUST TO AVOID

Following on from grammatical errors come words that are commonly misused, through carelessness or ignorance, and words and expressions which, for a variety of reasons, are best avoided. Some of them are simply incorrect, others are clichés and still others are pieces of jargon from the business world or the psychiatrist's couch. Tautology – accidentally saying the same thing twice – has a section of its own at the end of the chapter, but examples of this may also be considered chronic stumbling blocks.

No-one who aspires to Elegant speech should ever be in such a hurry to finish a sentence that they have to use ugly expressions for the sake of brevity. On the other hand, modern English is being infiltrated by some extraordinary – and certainly Inelegant – circumlocutions (see *At this moment in time,* below), by meaningless 'fillers' and by fatuous examples of political correctness. While Her Ladyship is all in favour of avoiding language that unthinkingly reinforces stereotypes, such as *Englishmen* when the entire race is meant, she resolutely holds out against extreme forms of this phenomenon.

> **No-one who aspires to Elegant speech should ever be in such a hurry to finish a sentence that they have to use ugly expressions for the sake of brevity.**

Stumbling blocks and interlopers

acute/chronic

Referring to an illness or complaint, *chronic* does not mean severe; it means deep-rooted and long-lasting. The opposite is *acute*, which means short-lived and probably severe. Thus *chronic* eczema may not normally give much trouble but one may occasionally suffer an *acute* flare-up.

actually

This is a very popular word that is almost always redundant: *I don't actually like tomatoes* is no different from *I don't like tomatoes*. *Actually* should be used only to stress the difference between something that is true and something that is not: *She said she was busy at the weekend, but **actually** she spent all Saturday watching television.*

advance/advanced

As an adjective, *advance* means 'ahead of the main body', 'forward in position or time'. *Advanced* means 'ahead in development, knowledge or progress', 'having reached a comparatively late stage', 'ahead of the times'. Thus one may receive an *advance payment* on money due, have one's secretary make an *advance booking* for a concert, be given *advance warning* of something that is going to happen in the future. Or one may pass *advanced level examinations*, have reached an *advanced age* or have *advanced views* on a particular subject. The common mistake here is to say something like *an advanced warning*, which would mean 'a particularly sophisticated warning given at an unspecified time' – probably not what the speaker intended.

advert

… is an item on Her Ladyship's list of pet hates. The word is *advertisement*.

(I'm) afraid to say

This tautology is creeping into common use and is an expression Her Ladyship deplores. One used simply to say *I can't come that day, I'm afraid* or *I'm afraid I don't agree with you*. There was (and is) no suggestion of fear – this was merely a polite way of softening a negative or mildly embarrassing statement. More explicit were *I'm sorry to say* or *I'm embarrassed to say*. Now the two forms seem – unnecessarily – to be being amalgamated.

alright

There is no such word. Whatever the context, *all right* should be two words.

among/between

Between is used for two things, *among* for more than two:

> *My husband and I can decide this **between** ourselves*
> *The director distributed the scripts **among** the members of the cast*

Amongst means the same as *among*, but is old-fashioned.

When naming the two things between which a choice is being made, the correct conjunction is *and:*

> *The war took place between 1939 **and** 1945* (not *1939 to 1945,* nor *1939–45*)
> *She had to choose between buying the bracelet **and** saving her money* (not *or saving …*)

anticipate

This does not mean 'expect', it means 'foresee and take appropriate action'. *He anticipated my question by explaining his intentions* is correct; *I am anticipating that he will arrive at 5 o'clock* is not.

any one/anyone

Anyone is a pronoun referring to 'any person': *Is **anyone** going to be kind enough to pour the tea?* Any one (or *any one of*) is what is technically called an adjectival phrase, used to describe a noun and meaning 'any single one': ***Any one** offer would have pleased me* or ***Any one** of the girls should have been able to lift a teapot.*

Similar rules apply to *every one/everyone* and *no one/no-one:*

> ***Every one** of you should be ashamed*
> ***Everyone** arrived in good time*
> ***No one** person could have done all that work*
> ***No-one** worked harder than she did*

Anybody, everybody and *nobody,* each written as one word, may be substituted for *anyone, everyone* and *no-one* in these contexts: *any body* etc. as two words emphasises the body rather than, say, the head or the mind, or suggests a corpse:

> ***Every body** was beautiful, every mind a blank*
> *The murder investigation was hampered by the fact that **no body** had been discovered*

apposite

This means 'suited for the purpose, appropriate', as in *The use of an **apposite** quotation illustrated the point well.* It has nothing to do with *opposite.*

arm candy

This is an expression that almost tempts Her Ladyship to go down on her knees. Without resorting to that drastic measure, she most earnestly begs her readers not to use it. She feels equally strongly about *eye candy.*

at the end of the day
This means – well, at the end of the day. In the evening. At night.
It does not mean 'In summary', 'When all is said and done' or
'Now I come to think about it'.

at this moment in time/at the present point in time
These both mean 'now', which is what one should say if that is
what one means. Similarly, the expression *in this day and age*
means 'nowadays'.

attendees/standees
The suffix *-ee* indicates that a person is the recipient of an action
– a *lessee*, for example, or a *licensee*, to whom a lease or a licence is
granted. The person performing the action is the *lessor* or *licensor*.
People attending a conference, therefore, are – if one really must
use the word – *attenders*, though *those attending* and *delegates* are
both more Elegant. Someone forced to remain standing on a
crowded method of public transport could be described as a
stander, but by no stretch of the imagination a *standee*.

BCE
No-one in Her Ladyship's circle uses this abbreviation. Whatever
one's religious beliefs, the years in the 'common era' are reckoned
from the supposed birth of Christ, so those preceding it are *BC*
– *Before Christ*. Until the Western world adopts another reference
point, it is absurd to attempt to disguise the origin of this method
of expressing dates. (Her Ladyship would also like to draw
attention to the care she took to avoid using the modern cliché
'benchmark' in the previous sentence.)

ballgame
The underrated musical *City of Angels* by Cy Coleman, David Zippel
and Larry Gelbart features a Hollywood producer much given to

colourful mixed metaphor along the lines of 'No-one gets a hole in one the first time they swing a racquet'. Another character, responding in kind, suggests, 'That's a ballgame of a different colour, right?' Right, indeed, says Her Ladyship, in a rare lapse into American colloquialism. A *ballgame* is a *game* played with a *ball*, specifically, in North America, baseball. As a synonym for 'situation' – *a different ballgame, a whole new ballgame* – it descended to the level of cliché long ago and richly deserves the sort of mockery quoted above. A ballgame, by the way, is played in a *ballpark* and there is no reason to use this word as if it meant *approximate*.

bored of

One is bored *with* something or *by* someone. *Bored of* is Inelegant and rather petulant.

borrow/lend

When one *borrows* something, one temporarily takes possession of it. When one *lends* something, another person has the use of it.

> *He **borrowed** money from the bank so that he could buy a new car*
> *The bank **lent** (or **loaned**) him the money*

Note that *loaned* almost always refers to money. One would *lend*, rather than *loan*, a lawnmower (or the gardener) to a neighbour so that he could mow the lawn. Although one may, in awkward circumstances, ask for a *loan* from the bank, neither *lend* nor *borrow* are nouns: *Could I have a lend* (or a *borrow*) *of your iPod?* is wrong.

can I get…?

… *a decaff latté*, perhaps. *May I have …* is what is meant and should be used. See *can/may*, page 51.

challenge

See *issues*, page 74. Supposedly politically correct circumlocutions such as *vertically challenged* or *follically challenged* should be avoided except for consciously humorous effect.

check out

One *checks out* of a hotel. In any other context, *check* is perfectly adequate. The invitation to *check out our website*, particularly if this is followed by an offer to *check out our great deals*, makes Her Ladyship squirm.

chill

Speaking of making Her Ladyship squirm, this is another expression that causes her great discomfort. *To chill* is to put something in the refrigerator; it is not to relax. The injunction *Chill!* meaning 'Don't make a fuss' should never be used when anyone over the age of seventeen is present.

closure

This word has a number of technical meanings when applied to such events as the closure of a debate in parliament or to things mathematical, logical or geological. As a piece of psychobabble meaning 'coming to terms with the end of a relationship' it is shunned by speakers of Elegant English. *Psychobabble* is becoming a cliché and should normally be shunned too, but in this sentence – if spoken with sufficient venom – it is the *mot juste* (see page 17).

cold slaw

… does not exist. No matter at what temperature one eats it, the salad is *coleslaw*, from the Dutch for cabbage.

coming from

… as in *I know where you're coming from*, is used too often to mean 'I understand what you are saying' or 'I see what you mean'. Either of these alternatives is preferable.

comprise/consist of

The ground floor of a house may *comprise* (or *be comprised* of or *consist of*) a drawing room, dining room, study, kitchen, cloakroom etc.; it does not under any circumstances *comprise of* the rooms.

convince/persuade

In British English one may either *convince* or *persuade* someone *of* something, but may only *persuade* him or her *to do* something:

> *I **convinced** (or **persuaded**) my daughter that her skirt was too short*
> *I **persuaded** her not to go out dressed like that*

*I **convinced** her not to* … is an Americanism.

crescendo

This comes from the Latin for *to grow* (the gerund form: see page 40) and in music means 'growing in sound', 'becoming louder'. *To reach a crescendo* in a piece of music would therefore mean to arrive at the point where one began to play more loudly. In a non-musical sense it is almost always incorrect: one may reach a *peak* or a *climax*, but not a *crescendo*. *Rising in a crescendo* is an ugly tautology. Which, now Her Ladyship comes to think of it, is a tautology in itself: tautologies are by definition ugly (see page 86).

curry favour

This odd-looking expression comes from the verb *to curry* meaning 'to dress leather' or 'to groom a horse'. It means to attempt to ingratiate oneself in order to gain approval, promotion, etc. The frequently heard *to carry favour* is wrong.

dearly

It is impossible to *miss someone dearly*, although one may well have *loved them dearly*. A person may be missed *sorely, dreadfully, desperately* or simply *a lot*.

decimate

This originally meant 'to destroy one in ten': in Roman times the technique of killing one man in ten was used to maintain discipline in the army when mutiny was rumoured. The sense has developed to mean something more like 'to destroy nine-tenths', but not 'to destroy utterly', which would be *devastate* or *annihilate*.

different

Different to and *different from* are equally acceptable; it is *different than* that causes offence – in British English it is simply wrong. The verb *to differ*, however, should always be followed by 'from':

> *I must beg to **differ from** your point of view*
> *His course of action **differed from** the programme laid out in the manifesto*

dilemma

This is a choice between two (and only two) unpleasant options. It should not be used as a substitute for 'difficult decision', particularly when the result of making that difficult decision may be a happy one. Deciding which political party to vote for may be a dilemma, assuming one believes that they are all as bad as each other; choosing which dress to wear for a party is not, except in the unhappy event that both dresses are old-fashioned and unflattering.

The expression *on the horns of a dilemma* originally emphasised the two-pronged nature of the problem, but is now little more than a cliché.

disingenuous

Disingenuous does not mean 'ingenious'; it means 'insincere while pretending to be sincere'. A public figure, for example, might be accused of being *disingenuous* if he claimed to want to spend more time with his family. See also *genius/ingenious*, page 109.

disinterested/uninterested

Contrary to popular belief, being *disinterested* is a good thing, particularly if one is a judge or a member of a jury. It means that one has no *interest* (in the sense of a business interest or the opportunity for gain) in the outcome and is therefore able to be impartial. *Uninterested* means not interested:

> A **disinterested** *interviewing panel will appoint the best candidate for the position*
> An **uninterested** *panel does not care whom it appoints*

effectively

This means 'in an effective manner': *the music effectively conveyed the tragedy of the ending*. If what is meant is 'more or less', the correct expression is *in effect*: *The opera is effectively over when the fat lady sings* is wrong – *in effect, more or less* or *almost* would all effectively serve the purpose here.

electric

… is not a noun. If it becomes necessary, one turns off the *electricity*.

enjoy

Like *chill* (see above), this has recently and insidiously crept into the language as a single-word command of extraordinary Inelegance. *Enjoy* is a transitive verb; thus one may be invited to *enjoy oneself, enjoy a meal, enjoy a holiday,* but not non-specifically and intransitively to *enjoy.*

enormity
… has nothing to do with size. *The enormity of a deed* is the awfulness of it; one could apply the word to the Holocaust, to a serious crime or to an action that was going to make a major and unpleasant change in someone's life. *Enormousness,* meaning 'vast size', does exist but is clumsy-sounding and therefore rarely used. Depending on the context, *vastness, hugeness* or *the sheer size of the problem* may be better choices.

ethnic
This is a legitimate adjective meaning 'relating to a group of people with racial, linguistic and other characteristics in common'. It is insulting to people of any race to use it to mean 'someone of a different race from me'.

fill the knowledge gap
A clumsy paraphrase that is more likely to confuse than to enlighten. 'Tell you something you don't know' is what is meant.

(a) fine-tooth(ed) comb
A *fine-tooth comb* is a comb with fine and presumably numerous, close-together teeth. Combing something with such an implement means going through it very thoroughly and finding the smallest particles that are hidden in it. Whether the expression is being used literally or figuratively, finding small particles is the purpose of the exercise. To say, as many people do, *a fine tooth-comb,* with the emphasis on 'tooth', either suggests that this is a particular sort of comb that happens to have teeth (as opposed to a comb that merely has gums, perhaps?) or conjures up a surreal image of an appliance used for combing teeth, perhaps as a replacement for *a tooth brush.* To omit the *fine* altogether and say *I went through it with a tooth comb* is even more absurd. If one were genuinely in such a hurry that leaving out a syllable was a matter of life and

death, the word to lose would be *tooth*: *a fine comb* (as opposed to a coarse one) is sensible enough.

fit
This means 'suitable for the purpose for which it is intended' or 'healthy, athletically toned'. It is not used in Elegant circles to suggest sexual attractiveness.

for free
This is never said by anyone who aspires to Elegance. One may go to an exhibition *free*, *for nothing* or, somewhat pretentiously, *gratis*, but not *for free*. If the exhibition happened to be a private view, a *complimentary* glass of wine might well be included, but again this is not to be had *for free*. See also *complement/compliment*, page 101.

fortuitous
... does not mean *fortunate*. It means 'happening by chance'. *A fortuitous meeting* might occur when one unexpectedly met someone in the street; one was not necessarily pleased to see that person.

fulsome
... is a pejorative word. *Fulsome praise* is not abundant, generous praise, it is excessive, insincere and given with a view to currying favour (see above).

get
Not so much misused as overused. Nine times out of ten a little thought will provide an alternative:

> *I could **be*** (not 'get') *there by eight o'clock*
> *What should I **buy*** (or ***give***, but not 'get') *her for her birthday?*
> *Let me **fetch*** (not 'get') *it for you*
> *When you **reach*** (not 'get to') *the main square, turn left by the church*

*She said she would **arrive** (not 'get here') in time for dinner*
*I normally **rise** (not 'get up') at 7 o'clock*

If it becomes essential to use this verb, the past tense and past participle are both *got*. In modern British English there is no such word as *gotten*, although the adjective 'ill-gotten' is still used.

going forward
... is a piece of management jargon that is insidiously gaining wider currency. Her Ladyship implores readers to say 'tomorrow' or 'in the future' if that is what they mean.

good
This is an adjective, and is therefore used to describe a noun or a pronoun (see page 29). *I'm good* means 'I am well behaved'.
It should not be used as a substitute for 'I am well, in good health' nor – and here Her Ladyship can barely suppress a shudder – for 'Thank you, but I do not require another drink at the moment'.
In both senses, *I'm OK* or *I'm fine* is acceptable only in the most casual of circumstances.

gutted
Fish are *gutted*, people are not, unless perhaps they are captured by cannibals or taken by a shark. There are many more Elegant ways to express sorrow, disappointment or chagrin. To claim to be *literally gutted* adds absurdity to Inelegance – see *literally*, page 77.

hanged/hung
People used to be *hanged*; pictures and meat are *hung*.

(not a) happy bunny
Circumlocutory and baffling (why rabbits in particular?), this cliché can be replaced with *not happy*.

hoi polloi

… means 'the common people'. *Hoi* is Greek for *the*, so *the hoi polloi* is wrong.

hopefully

Hopefully means 'full of hope'. The proverb *It is better to travel hopefully than to arrive* may or may not be true, but it is grammatically correct. **Hopefully** *you will enjoy this book* would be correct only if Her Ladyship knew that 'you' were reading it in a spirit of hopefulness. It is much more likely that she meant **I hope** *you will enjoy this book.*

hysterical

Hysterical means suffering from or exhibiting hysteria, which is – in the non-medical sense – a frenzied emotional state. The word should not be used as a synonym for *hilarious*. A person may be (permanently) *hysterical* by nature or (temporarily) *hysterical* with mirth or grief; their laughter or tears may equally be *hysterical*, but the situation which provokes *hysterical* laughter is not itself *hysterical*.

I have to say

See *with all due respect*, page 85.

I personally

This is really a tautology (see page 86), but is included here because it is also a piece of meaningless verbal padding. *I'll deliver the parcel personally* (meaning 'I shall take it myself rather than posting it') is perfectly acceptable, as is *I took her remarks personally* ('I was upset by what she said'). On the other hand, *I personally disagree with you* means nothing more than *I disagree with you.* For emphasis in speech – *Amy may say what she likes, but I think you are both wrong* – simply stress the 'I'.

ignorant

This means 'lacking in knowledge' or 'demonstrating a lack of knowledge'. One may be generally *ignorant* (meaning uneducated and uninformed) or *ignorant of the rules of bridge,* or one may make an *ignorant remark,* revealing that one knows little about the subject under discussion. But *ignorant* should not be used as a substitute for *ill-mannered.* An *ignorant* person is ill-informed, not necessarily badly brought up.

> **Ignorant *should not be used as a substitute for* ill-mannered.**

imply/infer

A speaker *implies* something – that is, suggests it without spelling it out. The hearer listens to what has been said and, with luck, *infers* what is meant.

*Am I to **infer** that you don't want to invite your mother for Christmas?*
*I didn't mean to **imply** anything of the sort*

incredibly

Another example of a word being trivialised and therefore weakened, as in *It was incredibly hot in the Turkish bath.* Turkish baths are routinely heated to something in the region of 43°C – there is nothing *incredible* about the fact that they are hot. *Very* or *extremely* would serve the purpose in this context.

irregardless

… is a non-existent word, an illiterate amalgam of *irrespective* and *regardless,* either of which should be used instead:

> *I intend to go **irrespective** of whether it rains or not*
> *It may or may not rain – I intend to go **regardless***

issues

Her Ladyship simply does not understand the modern aversion to the word *problem*. An *issue*, in addition to being a copy of a magazine or a formal way of referring to one's children, is 'a point on which a question depends, a point in dispute': *the point at* **issue** *is whether to drive or take the train* or *the* **issue** *is whether or not fee-paying schools promote snobbery*. To say that someone has *issues* with her parents is to undermine both the true meaning of the word and the seriousness of the problem. The same applies to *challenge*, which is 'a difficulty *that stimulates interest or effort*' (Her Ladyship's italics), not just any old difficulty.

item

An *item* appears on an agenda (see page 41) or a shopping list. Two people who are involved in a romantic and/or sexual relationship are a *couple*.

kindly

This is an adverb meaning 'in a kind way': *He treated me* **kindly** *and I am grateful to him*. It should not be used as a (slightly threatening) substitute for 'please', as in **Kindly** *leave that alone*.

(to have a) laugh

… is decidedly Inelegant. *To enjoy oneself* or *to laugh a great deal* is the Elegant equivalent. The more or less rhetorical question *Are you having a laugh?* should be replaced by *You must be joking* or, more specifically, *That is a ridiculous price/offer/suggestion*.

learn/teach

A student may *learn* a subject, or a lesson in life. A teacher *teaches* a subject, or *teaches* students, or *teaches* a subject to students. The one thing a teacher cannot do is *learn* students. Thus:

*The professor **teaches** French to mature students*
*Elizabeth is **learning** French*

are both correct;

*I'll **learn** him to talk to me like that*

is not.

lie/lay/laid/lain

Lay is a transitive verb; it needs an object in order to complete its meaning. One must lay *something*, whether it be a table or – if one is a bird – an egg. The past tense of this is *laid*:

*I **laid** my cards on the table*

The past participle is also *laid*:

*the hen had not **laid** any eggs when I looked this morning.*

Lie is intransitive, complete in itself. This is true whether one is lying to get oneself out of trouble or lying on one's bed. In the sense of telling an untruth, the past tense and past participle are both *lied*:

*You **lied** to me!*
*I can't believe he would have **lied** about something like that.*

In the sense of lying down, the past tense is *lay:*

*I **lay** there for an hour but nobody came in.*

The past participle is *lain: I would not have **lain** on the grass if I had realised that it was damp.*

75

like

This is one of the most overused and misused words in English –
and was, even before the distressing colloquialism *And I'm, like,
yeah, whatever* came into being. It is frequently used in place of *as,
as if* and *such as* in sentences such as:

> *As* (not *like*) *any young lady should know, black is a very ageing
> colour*

> *Even if you dislike your godmother's present, please say thank you
> as if* (not *like*) *you meant it*

> *Spring flowers such as* (not *like*) *daffodils and primroses always
> cheer me up*

In the last example, *Spring flowers like daffodils and primroses* means
flowers that *resemble* (i.e. *are like*) daffodils and primroses – perhaps
because they are yellow – but are specifically *not* daffodils and
primroses.

Similarly:

> *Shakespeare wrote tragedies such as* King Lear *and* Macbeth (*such
> as* gives examples of the tragedies)

> *Christopher Marlowe wrote tragedies like* King Lear *and* Macbeth
> (he didn't write the two plays mentioned, but he wrote
> others that resembled – i.e. *were like* – them)

listen

… is not a noun. It is Inelegant to ask someone to *have a listen to
this*. Or indeed to *have a read* of something. See also *borrow/lend*
(page 64).

76

literally

One of the most commonly misused words. A friend recently told Her Ladyship, rather alarmingly, that her two siblings were *literally chalk and cheese.* One is a slim, dark man; the other a solidly built woman with fair hair. They also have very different personalities. Metaphorically or figuratively, therefore, they are chalk and cheese. Literally, Her Ladyship can assure her readers, they are nothing of the sort.

To take another example, *The bomb literally destroyed the house* could well be true; *she was literally destroyed by the news* is unlikely to be, unless the news brought on a heart attack. *I was literally devastated* is absurd: either one was devastated or one wasn't, and the adverb adds nothing.

love interest
This expression may be tolerated (reluctantly as far as Her Ladyship is concerned) when it refers to a (usually female) character in a modern film whose function in the plot is to bed the (usually male) star. Used with reference to characters in the novels of Jane Austen or Mrs Gaskell, it plumbs the depths of Inelegance. So too, in any circumstances, does any pronunciation of *love* that approximates to *lurve*.

meretricious
... has nothing to do with *merit.* It derives from a Latin word for a prostitute and means 'superficially attractive but of no real value; flashy, insincere'.

methodology

This is a fairly technical word meaning 'the system of methods and principles used in a particular discipline', such as the way in which a scientific experiment is carried out. If this is not what is meant, *method* is almost certainly a better choice.

(a) mind of information

Though it is easy to see how this confusion arose, the correct expression is *mine of information, mine* meaning a deep, rich source, as in *a gold mine*.

mindset

'State of mind', 'fixed opinion', 'point of view' or 'attitude' all convey a shade of meaning that is absent from this word. They also convey the impression that the speaker has thought about what he or she wishes to say, rather than resorting to a trite and predictable piece of jargon.

momentarily

This means *for* a moment, not *in* a moment: *The robin landed momentarily on the fence before flying off again.* The Americanism *I'll do it momentarily* is frowned upon in Elegant British society.

(that's a) no-brainer

This expression is now so overused that it has lost any shreds of originality it may once have had. *That's easy* or *That's no problem* are much more natural, unpretentious ways of saying the same thing.

no worries

Acceptable if one is Australian or a character in *The Lion King*, this should otherwise be replaced by *No problem* (in casual speech) or something more formal such as *Please don't mention it* or *I am happy to have been of service.*

noisome
This means 'offensive, disgusting' and is often applied to smells; it has nothing to do with *noise*.

(the) odd
In the sense of 'the occasional', this does not need to be qualified by a number. *I visited the odd stately home or two* is a tautology: use either *the odd stately home* or *a stately home or two*.

ongoing/on an ongoing basis
Another piece of jargon that is easy to avoid: try *the research is continuing; the investigation is still in progress; we expect work on this to carry on for some time*.

plunge
Plunging can be done downwards, on a level or metaphorically, so a swimmer may *plunge into the pool*, a ship may *plunge through choppy seas* and a philosophy student may *plunge into the works of Aristotle*. The over-enthusiastic leader of a walking tour who encourages his party *to plunge up the hill* is laying himself open to ridicule.

plus
… should not be used as a substitute for *as well as* or even *and*. *She had a busy weekend ahead: there was a party to go to, **plus** Rupert had asked her to dinner* is too informal for Her Ladyship's taste.

presently
… in British English means 'in a short while', not 'at present'. *He'll be home **presently*** is correct; *he is not at home **presently*** is not.

protest
Used transitively, this means much the same as *assert*: *He **protested** his innocence* means that he claimed he was not guilty. American usage

threatens to confuse this meaning: in Britain it is still essential to say, *He protested **against** ...* something to which one objects.

quietly confident
... is a cliché that smacks of self-satisfaction. *Confident* says the same thing without sounding complacent.

quote
... as a noun is always a less Elegant alternative to *quotation*: if one *quotes* from a poem, the words spoken are *a quotation;* a builder telling one how much a job is going to cost provides *a quotation* and 'this part of the sentence' is enclosed by *quotation marks.*

read
See *listen*, page 76.

(as) regards
In sentences such as *I should like to speak to you **as regards** the committee meeting*, this means 'about, concerning' and either of those words should be used instead. The same applies to *in regard to* and *with regard to*, both of which should be avoided. At the start of a sentence such as ***With regard to** the discussion at the committee meeting, I do not feel that any further action is necessary, with **reference** to* is what is meant.

regularly
... does not mean 'frequently', it means 'at regular – that is, evenly spaced – intervals'. One of Her Ladyship's cookery books contains the unhelpful instruction, *Transfer to the oven and cook for a further two hours, basting regularly.* Basting once an hour would be just as 'regularly' as basting every five minutes, but presumably what is meant is 'basting frequently'. Similarly, one often hears remarks such as *He was an attentive son – he visited his mother regularly.* That

might mean he visited her faithfully twice a week or that he went every year on her birthday but at no other time. The same remarks apply to visiting as to basting: an attentive son would visit his mother *frequently*.

sat
The present participle of the verb *to sit* is *sitting*. *Sat* is the past tense or past participle. Therefore *He **sat** on the sofa* and *He **had sat** down before he realised that everyone else was standing* are correct. *He **was sat** in the garden* is not.

scarify
This has nothing to do with *scare* and is sometimes used as if it did, presumably by analogy with *horrify* and *terrify*. *Scarify* is a word only a keen gardener need use: it means breaking up soil to help seeds take root, or scratching the outer surface of the seeds to assist germination.

scenario
A *scenario* is an outline of the plot of a play or film. Its overuse, in the sense of 'set of circumstances', should be avoided. *Worst-case scenario* is also a tautology – it means the same as *worst scenario* – and has become such a cliché that people now frequently abbreviate it to *worst case …*, knowing that their hearer will tacitly supply the final word. This is an instance where Her Ladyship acknowledges a losing battle, but she would be interested to know who first decreed that *If the worst happens* was an inadequate turn of phrase.

(in the) scheme of things
Like 'with a tooth comb' (see page 69), the omission of a word in order to save a fraction of a second reveals a poor understanding of what one is saying. *In the greater scheme of things*, although perilously

close to being a cliché, means 'taking a wider view, considering all aspects of a situation without becoming overwhelmed by detail'. Take out the *greater* and the result is meaningless.

seriously

This (obviously) means 'in a serious way, gravely, importantly, humourlessly' and should not be used as a synonym for *very*. Examples such as *If I don't go now I am going to be **seriously** late* or *She was wearing a **seriously** expensive-looking pearl necklace* trivialise what should be a serious word.

shampoo

… is for washing hair. As a synonym for *champagne* it may be jocular but it is hardly Elegant.

slip through the net

Another expression that might once have been original and lively but is now merely hackneyed. *This seems to have slipped through the net* means nothing more nor less than *I forgot*, which has the additional advantage of being honest.

squeeze

A hideously Inelegant description of the latest companion and presumed bedfellow of a famous or mildly famous person, to be avoided at all costs. *Companion* is the word required; nothing more about the relationship is anyone else's business.

steal/rob

If one is of a criminal bent, one *steals* a thing and *robs* a person (or a bank).

> *He **robbed** Peter to pay Paul*
> *He **stole** money from Peter so that he could afford to pay Paul*

suck
Another transitive verb whose intransitive use should be avoided in Elegant company. A person, thing or situation does not *suck* unless it has a straw in its mouth.

that
… should not be used when one means *so*: *He's **that** handsome he can be as selfish as he likes* is wrong on every possible level.

throes
It is debatable whether one should discuss *death throes* or *the throes of passion* or other violent emotion in Elegant society, but if the need to write about them should occur, they are spelt thus. The word, which is rarely used in the singular, has no connection with *throwing*, even if what is being thrown is a tantrum.

touch base
When telephoning friends for no specific reason, Her Ladyship might say, *I just wanted to see how you were* or … *say hello.* She would only ever *touch base* in the highly unlikely event that she were playing rounders.

transportation
Her Ladyship recently came across (in an American book, she is relieved to say) the word *punishmentation*, meaning *punishment*. The author was (Her Ladyship hopes) using this for comic effect, but it is a reflection of a phenomenon to be avoided. *Transport* is a perfectly acceptable word for 'a system for transporting people' (as in *public transport*); the world has no need for the word *transportation* now that convicts are no longer sent to Australia.

> **The world has no need for the word transportation *now that convicts are no longer sent to Australia.***

Something similar may be said about *bother* and *botheration*, although the latter is quite a satisfying exclamation in times of stress.

tribute
A *tribute* should be paid to someone who has died or, at the very least, retired after a long and distinguished career. When the English cricket team wins the Ashes, *congratulations* are more appropriate.

24/7
No-one with the slightest pretension to verbal Elegance ever uses this expression. *All day and every day, permanently* or *all the time* are infinitely preferable.

up to speed
Another piece of business jargon that is best avoided even in a business context. No-one is going to object to being brought *up to date* on a project or to being described as *well informed*.

well
Well does not mean the same as *very*. Sentences such as *She was well pleased with her new car* or *Years of experience had made him well familiar with the technique* are unquestionably Inelegant. In the first instance, *very* or *extremely* would be correct; in the second, *perfectly* or *quite* are also possibilities.

whence
Now used only in formal or archaic writing, this means 'from what place, cause or origin'. The key to its use – or misuse – is that it already contains the meaning of 'from': *Put that back from whence it came* is either tautological or *refained* (see page 11) and to be avoided in either case.

whether

This should not be used as a synonym for *if*. *Whether* is correct only when an alternative is presented:

> *Henry asked **if** (not **whether**) we would be at Ascot this year*
> *He also wanted to know **whether** we preferred champagne or Pimm's*
> *He said he would go **whether or not** we were able to join him*

window of opportunity

The next time you find this expression on your lips, dear Reader, Her Ladyship begs you to consider whether the words 'window of' add anything whatsoever to what you are trying to say.

with all due respect/I have to say/I must say

These are all expressions that typically precede an insult. *With all due respect, I disagree with every word you say* is not very respectful; *I have to say* (or *I must say*) *that dress doesn't suit you* is something that does not have to be said. Elegant speakers use none of these.

world war

Any British person of an age to remember the Second World War calls it the *Second World War* (or merely *the War*, though this is becoming dated as that generation passes on); World War Two (often written World War II) is an Americanism whose infiltration of British English should be resisted. The First World War should always be so called, whether one is of an age to remember it or not; the term *the Great War* also has a dated ring. The ugly abbreviations *WWI* and *WWII* suggest that the writer is in too much of a hurry to pay these pre-eminent world events the respect they are due.

Too much of a good thing

Appropriately enough, there are several technical terms for the common error of saying the same thing more than once. *Tautology, pleonasm* and *redundancy* all mean unnecessary repetition of the same idea and all mark the user as someone who has not thought clearly about what he or she is saying. Tautologies can also cause bafflement: Her Ladyship's online banking service offers something that it calls *an immediate faster payment,* and it is anyone's guess what that means.

The three most frequent mistakes here are restating the obvious, being confused by an acronym and overindulging in prepositions.

Restating the obvious

Expressions such as *safe haven, work colleague, intuitive instinct, unsubstantiated rumour* and *main protagonist* are all nonsenses: a haven is by definition safe; a colleague is someone with whom one works; an instinct cannot be other than intuitive; once a rumour is substantiated it ceases to be a rumour; a protagonist is always a principal character.

To identify these expressions and learn to avoid them, consider what the alternative would be: if the opposite is a contradiction in terms (or sounds absurd), then the chances are that one is guilty of tautology. *A dangerous haven, a play colleague, an acquired instinct, a confirmed rumour, a minor protagonist?* Her Ladyship thinks not.

The late Douglas Adams subtitled his novel *Mostly Harmless* 'the fifth book in the increasingly inaccurately named Hitchhikers Trilogy', because he knew that a *trilogy* consisted of three parts. (Other *tri-* words having to do with 'three' include *triple, triplet, triathlon, tripartite* and *triptych.*) He would presumably have winced at the inelegance of the commonly heard *three-part trilogy.*

Here are some other examples of tautology:

First originated: this suggests that it is possible to originate for a
   second time, which is clearly nonsense.
Universal panacea arises because the speaker is not aware that the
   prefix *pan-* comes from the Greek for 'all' (think of *pandemic*,
   a very widespread disease, and *panorama*, a view all around).
   A *panacea* by definition cures *all* ills – though it may be an
   exaggeration to claim that it does so throughout the known
   universe.
To return again means 'to return for at least a second time', that
   is, to visit for at least a third time. If one is simply going back
   to a place one has left, *return* or *go back* is all that is required.
She has an exciting future in front of her. Where else would her
   future be? Either *She has an exciting future* or *She has an
   exciting career in front of her.*
Reversing backwards? Again, Her Ladyship does not think so.

Also creeping into the language (and to be avoided) are expressions
such as *5pm this afternoon*. *Am* and *pm* come from the Latin for
'before midday' and 'after midday'. So, *5pm* is by definition in the
afternoon. *Five o'clock this afternoon* is correct; so is *5pm today* or *5pm
tomorrow*, but not *5pm this afternoon*.

Acronyms
An acronym is a pronounceable word, usually made up of the
initial letters or syllables of an organisation's name or of a set
phrase – thus NATO (for the North Atlantic Treaty Organisation)
is an acronym, because it is pronounced 'nay-toe'; the FBI
(Federal Bureau of Investigation) is merely an abbreviation (see
page 42). Strictly speaking, therefore, HIV is not an acronym,
because it is pronounced 'aitch eye vee' rather than 'hiv'. But it is

admitted in the following examples because it is such a frequent victim of the tautological phenomenon under discussion.

Consider the all-too-frequently heard Inelegancies *a PIN number* and *the HIV virus*. What does the speaker think the *N* and the *V* stand for? In the publishing world each book is allocated a unique *International Standard Book Number* and this is, understandably, almost always abbreviated to *ISBN*. Yet even within this supposedly literate profession one often comes across references to an *ISBN number*.

Prepositions

Prepositions (see page 31) are little words such as *at, to, under, on, off,* used to show where one thing is in relation to another, and it is a common mistake to use too many of them:

> *She was appointed to head **up** the enquiry*
> *She took a day off **of** work*
> *Put that book back **down** on the table*
> *The appointment of another director freed her **up** to take on*
>   *a more strategic role*
> *You mentioned him earlier **on** in the conversation*

Or, the favourite of television announcers:

> *Next **up**, after the news*

The words in bold are all unnecessary. The guideline is: if omitting a preposition doesn't change the meaning, take it out.

Outside and *inside* are of particular interest here. When used as prepositions themselves, they are frequently accompanied by the redundant preposition *of,* as in the Inelegant:

*A crowd gathered outside **of** the hall*
*Inside **of** the theatre, people began to take their seats*

However, both words can also be used as nouns, meaning *the exterior* or *the interior,* and in that case may be followed by *of.* These different uses can supply subtle differences of meaning:

*I can see snow **outside** the window* suggests that the snow may be lying on the lawn or on the driveway – the exact position is not specified
*I can see snow **on the outside of** the window* means that the snow is on the glass itself

A special case

Equally should not be followed by *as. Equally as interesting* is wrong. Use these alternatives instead:

I generally read The Spectator, *but find* New Scientist **equally interesting**
New Scientist *is (just/every bit)* **as interesting as** The Spectator

Finally, just plain wrong are *the reason is because* and *fairly unique.* Like the other expressions in this section, *the reason is because* says the same thing twice. Use *the reason is that …* or *It happened because …*

Unique comes from the Latin for *one,* and it means that there is only one of the thing being described. Thus it is possible for something to be *absolutely unique* (there really is only one of it) or *almost unique* (there might be two or three), but not *fairly unique, very unique* or *a bit unique.*

BIA: Beware Insidious Americanisms

The amoeba-like spread of television and the internet has exposed the world to American vocabulary and usage to such an extent that British English is in grave danger of surrendering its independence. So Her Ladyship beseeches her readers, if they are attempting to speak Elegant English, to *Beware Insidious Americanisms* and avoid them whenever possible (she would have preferred to say *Beware Rampaging Americanisms*, but felt that the resulting acronym was an unhappy one):

Use	Avoid
appeal against a decision	*appeal a decision*
at the weekend	*on the weekend*
film	*movie*
flat (a place to live)	*apartment*
cinema	*movies*
expand the business	*grow the business*
gain access to	*access*
had an impact on	*impacted*
lift	*elevator*
meet	*meet (up) with*
mobile (phone)	*cell (phone)*
pay rise or *salary increase*	*raise*
post, post-box	*mail, mailbox*
puncture	*flat*
put pressure on, pressurise	*pressure*
taxi	*cab*
trousers	*pants*
write to a person	*write a person*

In British English *a vet* is a veterinary surgeon. Someone who served in the Vietnam War is *a Vietnam veteran.*

Nounspeak

This useful term seems to have been coined by the American journalist Bruce Price to refer to such expressions as *increased market labour participation rates*, which means 'more people working'; *consumer discontent*, an abstract and therefore somehow blame-avoiding alternative to 'discontented consumers'; and *airplane delivery systems*, which may be bombs. The worst example that Her Ladyship has encountered is on the BBC's website, where a news item is headed *Cell death mark liver cancer clue.*

While the pernicious use of jargon in the first examples is to be deplored, the agglomeration of nouns at the expense of verbs, adjectives and even prepositions in the BBC headline goes beyond jargon to obscure meaning altogether. A clearer version might have been *Death marks on cells provide a clue to the causes of liver cancer*, but *death marks* remain mysterious: reading the article reveals that a protein that causes liver cancer is able to 'tag cancer-preventing cell machinery' with a view to destroying it.

Even this 'translation' contains examples of the modern obsession with agglomerating nouns. *Liver cancer* is *cancer of the liver*, while *cell machinery* is *machinery within the cells* – and still one might feel that *machinery* was an oddly automated word and that *organisms* might be more appropriate.

This noun-overuse phenomenon – or, as Her Ladyship would prefer, *phenomenon of the overuse of nouns* – is evident in many aspects of modern life: the sign *access toilet* is to be seen in at least one theatre in the West End of London. Clearly *disabled toilet* is deemed unacceptable and *wheelchair-accessible* too long for the space available, but the correct adjective to describe a toilet (or lavatory – see page 13) in this context is *accessible*.

Variations on this theme are also much in evidence:

• The concept that 'any noun can be verbed' may be gaining currency, but it will be admitted to Elegant English over Her Ladyship's dead body. Book-review sections of newspapers frequently announce that X has *authored* three previous books in a series. To Her Ladyship's way of thinking he has done no such thing. X *is the author* of them or *has written* them. Similarly, *critique* should be used only as a noun: *to write a **critique** of something* is *to review it, to analyse it*, but not *to **critique** it*.

• The ugly *to be sidelined* has come to mean 'to be unable to participate in a sport because of injury or disciplinary action', where surely *left on the sidelines* or *ruled out* would serve the purpose admirably. Her Ladyship recently heard *sidelined* used of an injured Formula One driver, unable to compete for the rest of the season in a sport whose terrain, so far as she is aware, does not have sidelines.

• Business jargon has turned *to progress* into a transitive verb: *At the next meeting we should discuss how to **progress** this*. Among speakers of Elegant English, this would be *We should discuss how to **advance** this project, to **move this project forward** or to **make progress** in this area*. See BIA (page 90) for more examples of this American infiltration.

• Verbs such as *burglarise* are created by those who seem unaware of the existence of the word *burgle*, which has a long pedigree and does not deserve to fall from favour. Even worse are *diarise* for 'to note a date in one's diary', 'to make an appointment' or *circularise* instead of 'to send out a circular'.

Her Ladyship had written the previous paragraph before reading a newspaper report about a new manual that aims to teach basic grammar to teachers who may not have learned it at school. Punctuation, it explains, is used to 'chunk text up into meaningful units'. *Diarise* and *circularise* pale into insignificance alongside the horror of *to chunk*.

4

CONFUSABLES

English is full of words that look and sound confusingly alike, but have completely different – or subtly different – meanings. Yet distinctions – even the subtle ones – are worth preserving. Speakers of Elegant English should never have to say, 'Well, you know what I mean' because, through a careful and accurate choice of words, they will have said exactly what they mean.

Distinctions – even the subtle ones – are worth preserving. Her Ladyship's most important rule of vocabulary is 'Do not use a word unless you are sure of both its meaning and its pronunciation'. Anyone who does not follow this advice and 'gets it wrong' will look as if they are trying to impress – and will impress nobody.

acetic/ascetic/aesthetic
Acetic (pronounced 'a-seat-ick') acid is vinegar and the adjective is rarely used other than in this literal sense. *Ascetic* ('a-set-ick') as a noun means a monk or other person who practises self-denial; the adjective means 'abstemious, austere' and may describe either a person or a lifestyle. *Aesthetic* ('ees- or ess-thet-ick') means pertaining to beauty or taste, and often has overtones of pretension: Oscar Wilde, for example, was described as an *aesthete* by those who disapproved of him; to describe the décor of a room as *aesthetically pleasing* would almost certainly be considered patronising by the decorator.

adverse/averse

Adverse means 'unfavourable, hostile' as in *adverse weather conditions* or an *adverse criticism* – the sort of remark that might be made by an *adversary*. *Averse* means 'unwilling' and is often used in the negative: *He was not **averse** to the suggestion* means that he was happy to agree, he felt no *aversion*.

affect/effect

Affect is a verb, *effect* is usually a noun: *I **affected** (i.e. altered) the outcome by having an **effect** on what people thought*. *To affect* can also mean to assume, to pretend: *I **affected** a careless manner so that she wouldn't know how upset I was*.

To effect means to bring something about, usually a change: *The only way to **effect** a change in government is to vote for someone else*. See also *effectively*, page 68.

aggravate/annoy

To aggravate means to make something worse: one may, for example, *aggravate a situation* by tactless behaviour, and doing so may *annoy* those concerned.

aid/aide

An *aide* is a person employed to provide *aid*. A *teaching aide* might help the qualified teacher in the classroom; either could use *teaching aids* in the form of books, DVDs and the like.

allay/alley/alloy/ally

Four words that are not connected in any way but by the similarity of their spellings: *to allay* (pronounced 'a-lay', with the emphasis on the second syllable) is to relieve or reduce an emotion, as in *Her calm words helped to **allay** his fears*. An *alley* ('al-ee', emphasis on the first syllable) is a passageway or narrow lane; also, Her Ladyship is reliably informed, a venue for ten-pin bowling. An *alloy* ('al-oy', emphasis on the first syllable) is a metallic substance produced by mixing two or more others, such as brass, which is a mixture of copper and zinc. An *ally* ('al-eye', emphasis on the first syllable) is someone who is connected to or on the same side as another. With the emphasis on the second syllable this becomes a verb: one may be *allied* to someone in marriage or as the result of a political treaty. *The Allies* with an initial capital generally refers to the countries that fought against Germany, Italy and Japan during the Second World War; that is, Britain, France, the Commonwealth nations, the United States, the Soviet Union and others.

alternate/alternative

Both words come from the Latin meaning 'the other one (of a choice of only two)', but *alternate* applies to two things taken turn and turn about, while *alternative* is a second choice, something different from the first selection:

> *A dum-di-dum-di-dum rhythm places the stress on **alternate** beats*
> *If you do not care for salad, lightly steamed vegetables are*
> *a healthy **alternative***

amoral/immoral

Amoral means 'having no moral quality, outside the realms of morality'; *immoral* means 'breaking the rules, not conforming to conventional moral standards'. Thus some sciences or scientists may be considered *amoral*, because they pursue knowledge regardless of the consequences. An *immoral* scientist, on the other hand, may be one who uses his knowledge to prepare an illegal drug or dissolve the lock on the door of a bank.

appraise/apprise

To appraise is 'to assess, to decide the worth of', whether making a formal valuation for tax purposes or attempting to sum up a person's character. *To apprise* is 'to inform' and is rather pseudo-formal, a word that might be put into the mouth of a butler in a mediocre costume drama: *I shall **apprise** Her Ladyship of your arrival, sir.* It is best avoided in non-satirical contexts.

assure/ensure/insure

The clear differences in meaning between these three words are probably best illustrated by an example: *By **insuring** his car, Francis **ensured** that he would be able to pay for repairs if he had an accident. As a result, he **assured** his worried mother that everything would be all right.*

aural/oral

Aural pertains to the ear; *oral* pertains to the mouth. One would have an *oral* examination (pronounced *o-ral*, with a short *o* as in *hot*) at the dentist, an *aural* one (pronounced *oar-ral*) if one were worried about one's hearing and possibly an *aural/oral* one if studying a foreign language. Her Ladyship advises readers to be particularly careful with this pairing: she recently heard one highly educated television presenter talking about something that sounded very like *aural sex*, which conjured up some shocking images.

avoid/evade/prevent

To *evade* something means to *avoid* it, but with the added implication that there is something dishonest or even illegal in the action. Tax *avoidance* may be achieved by giving gifts up to a specified legal maximum; tax *evasion* means finding ways of not paying what is owed. *Avoid* also does not mean the same as *prevent*: it is wrong to say *Her apology **avoided** an unpleasant argument.*

bail/bale

If a boat is filling with water, one *bails* the water out. The money paid to release someone from prison while they await trial is *bail*, and the metaphorical expression *to **bail** someone out,* meaning to help them out of trouble, is spelt thus. On the other hand, hay is bundled into *bales* and one *bales* out of an aircraft or out of a situation in which one no longer wishes to be involved.

born/borne

Both are past participles of the verb *to bear,* but are used in different senses. Almost anything that is carried, conveyed or supported is *borne,* whether it is a cartload of vegetables being *borne* to market, a (metaphorical or physical) cross that is *borne* on one's back or a grudge that is *borne* against another person. The principal exception arises when a woman *bears* a child, in which case the child is *born.*

bought/brought

Bought is the past tense and past participle of *to buy; brought* serves the same functions for the verb *to bring.* So *He **bought** me a present* may well be true, but *He **bought** me a present when he came to dinner* is almost certainly not: it is much more likely that he *brought* a present when he came to dinner, having *bought* it previously. And while on the subject, there is no such word as *brung. He **brung** me a present* is perhaps more Inelegant than any other example in this book.

brassiere/brasserie/brazier

The feminine undergarment has three syllables – '*braz*-ee-er' or (sticking more closely to the original French) '*braz*-ee-air'. The two-syllable 'bra-*zeer*' is to be discouraged. If in doubt, use *bra* or avoid the topic altogether. A *brasserie* ('*brass*-er-ee', with a short *a* as in *cat*) is a type of restaurant; a *brazier* ('*bray*-zee-er') is a form of heater. None of these words should elicit a giggle from either speaker or hearer.

breach/breech

All senses to do with breaking are spelt *breach*: a *breach* in a castle's defences, a *breach* of promise, a *breach* of the peace, a whale *breaching* the surface of the ocean. *Breech* is rarely found in the singular unless one is talking about part of a gun, or a *breech birth* when the unborn child is positioned wrongly; *breeches* are trousers ending at the knees.

broach/brooch

Both are pronounced with a long *o* as in *blow*, but a *brooch* is a piece of jewellery, while *to broach* a subject is to enter on it, to introduce it into conversation for the purposes of discussion (and possibly argument).

cache/cachet/cash

Cash is money in the form of notes or coins, as opposed to a cheque or stocks and shares. A *cache* (pronounced 'cash', from the French for *to hide*) is a store, a treasure that is hidden away. *Cachet* (pronounced 'cash-eh') means prestige or distinction: when Her Ladyship was walking in an African rainforest and had to take a detour because a poisonous spider had woven its web across her path, she felt this lent a certain *cachet* to the expedition.

canvas/canvass

Canvas is the material used by a painter or a tent-maker. *Canvassing* is done by politicians or their supporters in an attempt to solicit votes, or by opinion pollsters to assess the public's views.

caveat/caviar

Caveat (three syllables, 'cav-ee-at') is Latin for 'let him beware' and means 'a warning', particularly against over-optimism: *The initial results were promising but the researcher issued a **caveat** that they were as yet inconclusive.* The expression *caveat emptor* means 'let the buyer beware' and is a warning against making any purchase without first checking the quality of the goods; since a change in English and Welsh law forced the seller of a property to take more responsibility for its condition, *caveat vendor* is now also heard. None of this has anything to do with *caviar* (sometimes also spelt *caviare*), which is the smoked sturgeon's roe served as an hors d'oeuvre.

censor/censure

To censure is 'to condemn, to criticise severely'. A *censor* is a person employed by a prison or the armed forces to read letters and excise anything inappropriate, or by the British Board of Film Classification to watch films, decide for whom they are suitable and, again, cut out anything that they feel nobody should see. There is a verb *to censor*, which describes this action, and the derived noun is *censorship*. A *censer*, by the way, is a container for burning incense.

check/cheque

A *cheque* is the now nearly extinct piece of paper with which one authorises someone else to take money from one's bank account. Every other sense – *checks* and balances, a *checked* pattern on a tablecloth, *checking* whether the turkey is cooked – is spelt *check*.

chord/cord

Chords are musical, mathematical or emotional; *cords* are made of rope or similar material, or are put together in such a way as to resemble rope. Thus something one vaguely remembers may strike a *chord;* the human body has vocal *cords* and a spinal *cord*. Trousers made from *corduroy* are also *cords*.

cite/sight/site

All three of these words are pronounced in the same way, but they have completely different meanings. *To cite* is 'to quote, to give as an example'. One might, perhaps, *cite* the example of Henry VIII as one who married in haste and repented at leisure. A quotation

from the works of an author might be called a *citation;* this is also
the commendation given to members of the armed forces for acts
of outstanding bravery. A *sight* is something that is seen: visiting St
Paul's Cathedral and the Old Bailey might be described as *seeing
the sights* of the City of London; *sight* is also the sense of vision. *To
site* is 'to position something in a specific place': *The manor house
was **sited** in an attractive park.* This word may also be used as a noun:
the place where a building is *sited* is a *site; building sites* and
archaeological sites are also spelt this way.

complement/compliment

To complement means to match, to go well with – in terms of taste or
colour, for instance, or to make up a set: coriander and cumin
complement each other in a Moroccan dish; eight rowers and a cox
make up the full *complement* of a team for the Boat Race.
To compliment means 'to pay a compliment' – to say something
pleasant or flattering: *May I **compliment** you on your new hairstyle?*
    There is a similar distinction between the adjectives
complementary and *complimentary. Complementary* describes
something that goes with something else, balancing or completing
it: *complementary medicine,* for example, is used in tandem with
conventional medicine, not as an alternative to it. *Complimentary*
may mean 'pleasant, flattering', as in a *complimentary remark;* or it
may mean free, given with someone's *compliments: complimentary
coffee and cake* may be provided after a lecture, though of course
this really means that it is included in the price of the ticket.

confident/confidant(e)

Confident is an adjective meaning 'secure in one's knowledge
or position'. A *confidant* is a person in whom one confides, the
addition of the *e* indicating that it is a female. The final syllable of
confidant(e) is pronounced as in French – more *ont* than the
English sound *ant.*

conscientious/conscious

Conscious means 'awake' or 'aware', as in *He hadn't the strength to move, but he was still **conscious*** or *Everyone looked uncomfortable and I was **conscious** of having interrupted an argument*. *Conscientious* means 'painstaking in the execution of a task or duty', as in *a **conscientious** student* (one who always completes assignments on time) or 'obedient or loyal to conscience, governed by a sense of duty' as in a ***conscientious** objector* (one who refuses to go to war).

continual/continuous

The meaning of these two words is frequently blurred, but strictly speaking *continual* means happening over and over again, while *continuous* means never stopping. Thus one might be *continually* irritated by the noise made by the neighbours (because they had a party every Friday night), but *continuously* irritated by the humming of the refrigerator (because it literally never stopped).

corps/corpse

Corps (pronounced *core* in the singular, *core* or *cores* in the plural) comes ultimately from the same Latin root as *corpse*, a dead body, though it passed through French on the way, hence its pronunciation. A *corps* is a military body with a specific function, such as the *medical corps*, or any other organised group of people, such as the *diplomatic corps* or, reverting to the word's French roots, a *corps de ballet*.

credible/credulous (and incredible/incredulous)

All are from the Latin for 'to believe' but *credible* means 'able to be believed' and *credulous* 'likely to believe anything, without requiring evidence'. Thus a *credulous* person may be lured into believing an *incredible* story, which someone else might greet with an *incredulous* exclamation.

definite/definitive

Definite means 'clearly defined, exact'; *definitive* means 'conclusive, providing the final, decisive answer'. If Her Ladyship gives *a definite answer* to a question, her audience will be in no doubt as to her opinion, but she may be mistaken and she may change her mind tomorrow. If she gives *the definitive answer*, that is an end of the matter – there is no need for further enquiry.

defuse/diffuse

To defuse (pronounced 'dee-*fewze*') is to 'take the fuse out of something', literally or metaphorically. Thus one might *defuse* a bomb or *defuse* a potentially 'explosive' situation by the exercise of tact. *To diffuse* ('diff-*uze*') is 'to spread about, to scatter' and the adjective *diffuse* ('diff-*use*') means 'scattered over a wide area' or (of a speech, for example) 'covering a lot of subject areas, not all of them relevant'.

derisive/derisory

Derisive means 'expressing derision or contempt'; *derisory* is 'causing derision'. Thus a low opening bid at an auction might be *derisory* and be greeted by a *derisive* snort from an ill-mannered auctioneer.

discreet/discrete

A *discreet* person is one who can be trusted with a secret; a *discrete* section of a book is separate from the others, self-contained. Someone who is sleeping in a *discrete* part of a hotel may have to go outside and cross the garden in order to reach the dining room; in a *discreet* part, they would be entitled to expect privacy.

draft/draught

A *draft* is an outline of a contract or similar document, or an author, artist or architect's first attempt at a project, intended for discussion and amendment before the final version is produced.

It may also be a sort of cheque, as in *a banker's draft*. Being conscripted into the US Army is *the draft* and the word can be used as a verb in all these senses. The wind blowing into a room may create a *draught*, causing discomfort to anyone sitting playing the game of *draughts*. *Draught beer*, a *draught horse* and, confusingly, a *draughtsman* or *-woman* – one who produces scale drawings of a building or design – are all spelt this way.

egregious/gregarious
Both these words come from *grex*, the Latin for a flock of sheep, but the similarity between them ends there. Pronounced 'ee-*gree*-jus', *egregious* means 'standing out from the crowd', usually in a bad way: *an **egregious** example of an extravagant expenses claim*. *Gregarious* means 'fond of company, sociable'.

elegy/eulogy
An *elegy* is 'a mournful or plaintive poem', especially a lament for the dead. The most famous is Gray's *Elegy Written in a Country Churchyard*, in which the poet regrets 'the passing day' and all the 'mute inglorious Miltons' who may be buried nearby. Although a *eulogy* is frequently spoken at a funeral, its derivation is completely different (it comes from the Greek for 'good words') and it means a poem or speech not of mourning but of praise.

emigrate/immigrate
The prefix *im-* in this instance means 'in, into', so *to immigrate* is to migrate *into* a country. *E-* comes from *ex-* meaning 'out, away from' and *to emigrate* is to move *away from* a country. Thus a British person moving to New Zealand is *emigrating* from the UK and *immigrating* into New Zealand, where he or she will become an *immigrant*. *Emigrant* is most frequently used as an adjective in phrases such as *an emigrant worker* – that is, one working away from his or her home country. An *émigré* was a French aristocrat living

abroad having escaped arrest and execution during the French Revolution; the word is pretentious in any other context.

eminent/imminent

An *eminent* person is one who stands out from the crowd – *an eminent scientist,* for example, or (less likely nowadays, Her Ladyship fears) *an eminent politician.* An event rather than a person is *imminent*: it means 'likely to happen in the near future'. The consequences may be happy, as in *the imminent arrival of a baby,* or threatening, as in *an imminent disaster.*

endemic/epidemic

An *epidemic* disease affects a large number of people simultaneously, often spreading rapidly and causing serious illness or death, but lasting only a short time. An *endemic* disease is always present in a given area.

enquire/inquire

This is a nicety introduced into English specifically for the purpose of catching out the careless speaker or writer, or so it sometimes seems. *To enquire* is to ask in any informal sense; *to inquire* is to pursue a formal investigation. The same distinction applies to the nouns, *enquiry* and *inquiry.* Thus for the British Parliament to announce that *the Science and Technology Committee is to conduct an **inquiry** into scientific publications* is accurate, however soporific it may sound. A butler would be equally correct in saying to an unexpected visitor, *I shall **enquire** whether Her Ladyship is at home.*

epigram/epigraph/epitaph

An *epigram* is a short and witty saying of the kind popularised by characters in the plays of Oscar Wilde: 'In married life three is company and two none' or '[A cynic is] a man who knows the price of everything and the value of nothing'. An *epigraph* is a (preferably) brief and (preferably) apt quotation at the start of a book or a chapter of a book. An *epitaph* is the literal wording on a grave ('Here lies …'), or a tribute to the dead person.

equable/equitable

Equable (with the initial *e* short as in *get* and the emphasis on the first syllable) means 'even-tempered' when describing a person or 'unchanging' when describing a thing: *an **equable** climate* is not necessarily a mild one. *Equitable* (again with a short initial *e* and the emphasis on the first syllable) means 'just, fair', as in an ***equitable** division of the estate.* The adjective *equatable* ('eek-wait-able', with the emphasis on the second syllable) – from the verb *equate*, meaning to make or regard as equal – also exists, but is rarely heard outside mathematical circles.

exacerbate/exasperate

There is a parallel here to *aggravate* and *annoy* (page 95). One may *exacerbate* a problem (that is, make it worse) by behaving in an *exasperating* (annoying or irritating) manner. Be careful also not to confuse the central consonants: there is no such word as *exacerpate*.

exceptional/exceptionable

Exceptional is another word for 'standing out from the crowd'; *exceptionable* (more often used in the negative *unexceptionable*) refers to something to which one could *take exception* – that is, take offence or take a dislike. *An **unexceptional** Prime Minister* would be a run-of-the-mill one who resembled all the others; an ***unexceptionable*** one might be unique in that it was impossible to dislike him.

faint/feint

To faint is to swoon; the adjective means 'weak, feeble' in a number of senses: ***faint*** (cowardly) *heart never won fair lady; there was a **faint***

(slight, barely discernible) *glimmer of light in the eastern sky,
a **faint** sound coming from behind the door* or *a **faint** hope on the horizon.*
A *feint* means a mock attack designed to deceive one's opponent,
particularly in fencing or boxing; it may also be used as a verb:
*he **feinted** to the left and then delivered the final blow with his right hand.*
Additionally, a *feint* is a very faint line pre-printed on some types
of paper.

fare/fair

A restaurant may offer *a bill of fare; fares* must also be paid on
public transport. As a verb, *to fare* means 'to happen, to get on' –
hence the words *farewell, wayfarer* and *welfare.* The noun *fair* means
a gathering such as an *agricultural fair* or a *funfair;* the adjective
means 'just' – *He's a **fair** man; you can trust him to make the right
decision;* light-coloured, as in ***fair** hair;* or beautiful, as in ***fair** of face,*
although this usage is somewhat old-fashioned.

flounder/founder

A *flounder* is a flat fish and *to flounder* or *to flounder around* means
'to move with difficulty, to behave awkwardly, generally to be out of
one's depth' in either a literal or a metaphorical sense. An
incompetent swimmer may *flounder* in the water, for example; an
incompetent worker may equally *flounder around* in an office.
To founder, used literally, applies to a ship rather than to a fish and
means 'to sink'. Thus an overambitious project may *founder* – and
perhaps have *floundered* for a while first.

forbear/forebear

Any word prefixed with 'fore' is likely to be associated with
'before'. Thus a *forebear* (to be preferred to the inherently sexist
forefather) is one who has gone before, an ancestor. *Forbear* is a verb
meaning 'to refrain from': *I **forbore** to mention that I had heard this
story many times.*

forgo/forego

Similarly, *to forego* means 'to go before', most commonly used in the expression *a foregone conclusion*. *To forgo* is 'to give up, to do without': *I must **forgo** the pleasure of seeing you on Tuesday, as I shall be busy all day*. The expression *Forewarned is forearmed* also uses this sense of *fore-*, as do a weather *forecast*, a clairvoyant's *foretelling* of the future and a photographer's focusing on something in the *foreground* of a picture.

forward/foreword

The introductory section of a book is not a *forward*. It is a *word* (or number of words) that goes in the *foremost* part of the book, *before* the body of the text – a *foreword*. When *forward* occurs as a noun, it means a player in a rugby or football team; as an adjective it is used in contexts such as *the **forward** movement of the crowd*, **forward** *planning* or **forward** (i.e. impertinent) *behaviour*, as an adverb it refers to *moving **forward*** (as opposed to backward) or *sitting **forward*** (towards the front of an aeroplane or boat).

formally/formerly

There seems to be little confusion between the adjectives *formal* meaning 'pertaining to form, following a prescribed rule or convention' and *former* meaning 'previous, occurring at an earlier time'. Very few people would make the mistake of saying that someone had lodged *a **former** complaint*. Why, then, should Her Ladyship read – in, of all places, a magazine catering to the book trade – that one major company had *formerly* registered its objection to the activities of another? Frankly, she does sometimes despair.

funerary/funereal

Please be careful to give these words their full four syllables (the first is pronounced 'few' in both cases). *Funerary* means directly connected with a funeral or death: one may pay **funerary** *expenses*

or see a *funerary mask* in a museum. *Funereal* means *reminiscent* of a
funeral or death, as in *The black dress certainly made her look slimmer,
but the effect was somewhat funereal.*

genius/ingenious

Genius is not an adjective. Therefore, however much of a *genius*
a man might be, he cannot come up with *a genius solution* to a
problem. *An ingenious solution* would be a particularly inventive,
unusual one, suggesting that the solver had (to use an expression
that makes Her Ladyship cringe) 'thought outside the box'.
Otherwise, a solution might be *brilliant, clever, masterly* or any one
of a number of flattering adjectives (see also *disingenuous,* page 68).

gild/guild/gilt/guilt

To gild is to cover with gold or something golden; the result is a *gilt*
or *gilded* object. The famous *bird in a gilded cage* is in a cage painted
gold: luxurious but nonetheless a cage. This is also the sense (and
spelling) of *to gild the lily,* meaning to add unnecessary adornment.
A *guild* was a medieval professional association, as in the Guild of
Apothecaries or the Guild of Dyers; the word survives in this
context, and also describes similar organisations such as the
Townswomen's Guild. *Guilt* is the feeling of having done something
wrong, associated with *guilty.*

gourmand/gourmet

A *gourmet* appreciates good food and wine; a *gourmand* is
concerned with quantity rather than quality.

hoard/horde

The Mongol hordes who followed Genghis Khan would have
described themselves thus had they been writing about themselves
in English; and this is the spelling that means a large group of
people (*the hordes waiting outside the shop for the sales to begin*) or

animals (**hordes** *of ants crawling across the forest floor*). A *hoard* is a treasure or perceived treasure hidden (or *hoarded*) away for future use: a miser may *hoard* gold, while a thrifty housekeeper *hoards* empty jam jars. Large advertisements, particularly those by the side of the road, are displayed on a *hoarding*.

illegible/ineligible/intelligible

Easily confused because of similarities in sound, these three words have in fact nothing to do with each other. *Illegible* describes something that it is literally impossible to read, such as poor handwriting. It is not used metaphorically – a tiresome book may be *unreadable*, but it is *illegible* only if the type is too small. *Ineligible* means 'unable to be chosen'. One may be *ineligible* to join a golf club because one's play is not of a high enough standard, or *ineligible* for election because one does not live in the right county. *Intelligible* means 'able to be understood', so even the neatest and most *legible* print may be *unintelligible* to most readers if it uses jargon or technical vocabulary.

impractical/impracticable

An *impractical* solution is one that would be too expensive, take too long or in some other way be not worth the effort; an *impracticable* one cannot be carried out at all.

lama/llama

Lama is the priest, indigenous to Tibet; *llama* the animal, originating in South America.

lead/led

Lead (pronounced *led*) is a metal. *To lead* (pronounced *leed*) is to go ahead, to be the one in front. Its past tense and past participle are *led*: *Today I am **leading** a discussion, but yesterday I **led** …*

lightening/lightning

This is purely a matter of correct spelling, which is helped by correct pronunciation (of all three syllables in the first instance). *Lightening* is connected with the verb *to lighten*: the sun literally **lightens** *the sky* (making it less dark); a colleague may metaphorically **lighten** *one's load* (making it less heavy by sharing one's burdens). *Lightning*, the meteorological phenomenon that accompanies thunder, has only two syllables and no *e*.

liqueur/liquor

Liquor (pronounced 'licker') is any form of alcoholic spirit, or the juice in which food (especially fruit) has been cooked; a *liqueur* (pronounced 'lick-ure' or, in the French way, 'lee-kerr') is a sweet, after-dinner drink such as Grand Marnier or Drambuie.

loath/loathe

Loathe, loathing, loathsome are to do with hatred: *I **loathe** the sight of that man. He fills me with **loathing**; he is completely **loathsome**.* Loath (also sometimes spelt *loth*) means 'reluctant, unwilling': *I am **loath** to go away without alerting the police.* The expression *nothing loath* means 'perfectly happy', as in *I didn't think we would be able to find a way in but Bella, **nothing loath**, swiftly clambered up the drainpipe to the open window.*

loose/lose

This tends to be a spelling problem because in this instance the pronunciation is more of a hindrance than a help. *Loose*, which rhymes with *juice*, is the opposite of tight; *lose*, rhyming with *shoes*, means to misplace. *I'm loosing my mind* is therefore meaningless. *To loose* means to unfasten or untie, whereas *to loosen* means *to make looser* without necessarily unfastening altogether. In the unfortunate event of becoming insane one would be *losing* one's mind.

marquess/marquis/marquee

A *marquess* (with the stress on the first syllable) is a member of the British aristocracy, ranked below a duke. His wife is a *marchioness.* The use of *marquis* is increasingly widespread, but not to be indulged when one is addressing the peer himself. Strictly, a *marquis* (pronounced either '*mar*-quess' or in the French way, 'mar-*key*') is a nobleman of comparable rank from another country; notable examples include the Marquis de Sade (of sadism fame) or the Marquis of Carabas in the fairy tale 'Puss in Boots', both of whom were French. A *marquee* ('mar-*key*') is a large tent or awning normally erected in a garden to accommodate guests at a wedding or on the village green during a fête.

metal/mettle

A *metal* is certain kind of chemical element, most commonly a hard substance such as iron or lead. The adjective is *metallic,* as in a **metallic** *sheen* on a car's paintwork or a **metallic** *sound* as a saucepan falls on a slate floor. *Mettle* means courage or strength of character and is usually used in the expressions *to show* or *prove one's* **mettle**, meaning to demonstrate one's valour, or *to be on one's* **mettle**, to be ready to perform to the best of one's ability.

meter/metre

A *metre* is a unit of measurement (approximately 39.4 inches) and its various compounds – *centimetre, kilometre,* etc. – are all spelt this way. These are units in the *metric system. Metre* is also the spelling used in poetry, referring to the number of syllables in a line and the way they are stressed. A *meter* is an instrument used for measuring – *a gas meter, a parking meter, a barometer, a pedometer, a tachometer.* Confusingly, words such as *pentameter* and *hexameter,* indicating the number of feet in a line of poetry, are -*meter* rather than -*metre.*

minaret/minuet

Although they might be useful as the basis of a tongue-twister, these words are completely unconnected. A *minaret* is the tower on a mosque; a *minuet* is a stately dance or the music that accompanies it.

momentary/momentous

Momentary is the adjective from which *momentarily* (see page 78) is derived and means 'for a moment'. *I agreed out of **momentary** weakness* means the same as *I agreed **in a moment** of weakness. I agreed out of **momentous** weakness* would mean that the weakness was of great *moment* – that is, enormous, of great significance.

mooted/muted

Muted (first syllable pronounced 'mew') means 'silenced', both literally and figuratively, so that both a musical instrument and a response to a situation may be *muted*. *Mooted*, whose first syllable is the sound of a cow rather than a cat, means 'suggested, put forward for debate' and is connected to *a moot* (that is, debatable) *point*. The commonly heard expression *When the suggestion was first **muted*** is meaningless.

moral/morale

As an adjective, *moral* (pronounced with the stress on the first syllable) means 'pertaining to the difference between good and evil, conforming to accepted standards of behaviour' (see *amoral/immoral*, page 96). As a noun, it is the lesson to be learned from a story or an event: *The **moral** is, don't count your chickens before they're hatched. Morale* (stress on the second syllable) is a noun meaning 'condition or degree of strength of purpose, confidence, optimism, etc.'; it may be used in a military context to refer to *the **morale** of the troops,* or to *the **morale** of the workplace* in difficult times.

naught/nought

Naught means nothing, as in the expression *It all came to **naught***. *Nought* is the figure 0.

official/officious

Official means 'sanctioned by authority' or 'formal, ceremonial'. *Officious* means 'unnecessarily ready to offer advice or help'. Her Ladyship would certainly think twice about accepting an invitation to *an **officious** dinner*.

ordnance/ordinance

An *ordinance* is a decree, an order. *Ordnance* means military supplies, particularly artillery. The maps are produced by the *Ordnance Survey*.

pacific/specific

These seem to turn themselves into a tongue-twister for some people, but in fact there is no connection between them. *Pacific* is the name of an ocean and also means peaceful: *his **pacific** disposition was a blessing when the rest of the family came to visit*. *Specific* is connected with *species* and *specify* and means 'particular' or 'definite': *I can't give you a **specific** example; I just have a feeling about it*.

perspective/prospective

A *perspective* is 'a point of view' or 'a way of regarding situations, facts, etc. and judging their relative importance'. So, one might say, *From my **perspective**, this all seems rather trivial* – suggesting that other people are getting the situation *out of **perspective***. *Prospective* is an adjective meaning 'likely to happen in the future': an engaged man might have a conversation about his career *prospects* with his *prospective* father-in-law.

plain/plane

Plain is an adjective meaning 'simple, straightforward, unpretentious, not beautiful': *the **plain** truth, a **plain** answer, a **plain** woman* as opposed to a pretty one, *a **plain** fabric* as opposed to a patterned one. ***Plain** chocolate* has no milk in it; *a **plain-clothes** police officer* does not wear a uniform. As a noun, *plain* means a flat, probably treeless expanse of country, as in *The rain in Spain stays mainly in the **plain***. This is where the confusion frequently arises, because when one speaks of someone of great intellect as being on *a higher **plane***, one might expect the connection to be with a level piece of land. Not so: this sense of the word is associated with the mathematical *plane*, 'a flat surface, having only two dimensions'. A *plane* is also the tool used to level timber surfaces and *to plane* means to use such a tool. In addition, *plane* is a tree and an abbreviation for *aeroplane*.

pore/pour

One may *pore* over a book, but *pour* cream over profiteroles or complain that it is *pouring* with rain. The small openings in the skin are *pores*.

precipitate/precipitous

As an adjective, *precipitate* means 'rushing ahead', 'rash and premature'. So *a **precipitate** action* is one that is performed hastily, without enough thought. Although *precipitate* and *precipitation* are also nouns meaning moisture that has condensed and is now falling as snow or rain, for example, their use is best left to meteorologists: everyone else would be well advised to stick to the more direct *rain, snow, sleet* etc. *Precipitous* is related to *precipice* and simply means 'steep'; it is a prime example of the maxim that using a long word when a short one will do is likely to lead to embarrassment.

prescribe/proscribe

A doctor *prescribes* a medicine by writing a *prescription;* and note that it is *prescribe,* not *per-scribe. To proscribe* is to condemn, prohibit or exile.

prevaricate/procrastinate

To prevaricate means 'to speak or act falsely with intent to deceive', though it may be used in the sense of a white lie: *When she asked if he was planning a party for her birthday, he prevaricated.* It is not the same as *procrastinate,* which means 'to delay'.

principal/principle

Principal is an adjective meaning 'main' – a talented musician might be *the principal violinist* of an orchestra. As a noun it is commonly used in America to denote what in Britain is called the 'head' of a school; in Britain it may mean a person who engages another to act as his or her agent, or the original sum of money on which interest is calculated. A *principle* is standard of conduct or a firmly held belief: *He was a man of principle* (meaning he was honest and trustworthy) or *He objected to the change on principle* (because he did not want anything to change, not because there was anything wrong with the particular change in question).

prostate/prostrate

The first of these is unlikely to be mentioned in Her Ladyship's presence: it is a gland whose inflammation or malfunction causes gentlemen problems of an intimate nature. *Prostrate* means lying flat on the ground, face down (as opposed to *supine,* which is lying on the back).

pry/prise/prize

To pry is to take an inquisitive interest in something: *He is always prying into my affairs.* The third person singular is *pries,* which is one reason for the confusion with the other two words. The other may be blamed on *to prise,* which means to force open by levering or, figuratively, to extract with difficulty: one might *prise open* a treasure chest or *prise information* out of a taciturn person. The problem is that North Americans also use *to pry* in this sense. *To prize* is to value, and one wins a *prize* – perhaps for one's *prize* camellias at a horticultural show.

rack/wrack/wreck

A *rack* is anything on which items may be arranged, hung or displayed: *a coat rack, a shoe rack, a spice rack, a luggage rack* and so on. It is also the medieval instrument of torture, from which comes the verbal sense of 'to cause great suffering': *he was **racked** with guilt; she **racked** her brains to come up with a solution.* A *wreck* is a ship that has been destroyed at sea, or a person or thing in a similarly devastated condition: as a verb it means to destroy, and one may equally correctly (albeit carelessly) ***wreck** someone's car* or ***wreck** his chances. Wrack* is an archaic word whose meaning loosely overlaps those of the other two: it survived for a while in the expression *to go to wrack and ruin,* but this is now commonly spelt without the *w*. See also *reek/wreak*, below.

racket/racquet

A *racket* is a lot of noise, or a shady business deal. One plays tennis, badminton and the like with a *racquet*.

raise/raze

This is another pair of homophones ('sound-alike' words) that are frequently confused, the more so because they have opposite meanings. *Raise* means to lift or bring up, in a wide range of senses: one may ***raise** money, the alarm, a siege, one's hat* or *one's children. Raze* means to destroy something so thoroughly that the frequently used ***raze** to the ground* is a tautology.

reek/wreak

To reek is to smell, in the sense of 'to give off an unpleasant odour': an unhygienic kitchen might *reek* of yesterday's fish. *To wreak* (pronounced *reek*) means 'to inflict' and is most often used in such expressions as *to **wreak** havoc* or *to **wreak** a dreadful revenge.*

reign/rein

Reign is what a monarch does; a *rein* is used to control a horse or small child. *To **rein** something in,* therefore, is spelt thus and is connected with controlling a wayward animal or teenager, not exercising a royal prerogative.

role/roll

A *role* is a part played by an actor in a play, or an extension of that sense: *he played a leading **role** in the post-war Cabinet* or *the training course involved some embarrassing **role**-playing.* Insisting on the circumflex accent *(rôle)* is now rather old-fashioned and affected. In all other senses, including that of a list of names, the spelling is *roll,* hence *a **roll** call* and *a **roll** of honour.*

sceptic/septic

A *sceptic* (pronounced *skeptic*) is a person who doubts the truth of what he or she is told, whether it be conventional religion, political rhetoric or a daughter's promise to be home before midnight. The name comes from an ancient Greek school of philosophy, and the related adjective is *sceptical.* *Septic* is an adjective relating to pus and putrefaction, as in a wound that goes *septic* through not having been cleaned properly; or to *a **septic** tank,* used in rural areas as an alternative to mains sewage.

serve/service

Her Ladyship was shocked to hear a character on television (in, admittedly, an American drama) claim that her employer (the owner of an exclusive jeweller's shop) was *servicing* a client. In Her Ladyship's circles, a stallion *services* a mare and she believes that the local garage *services* cars. Most respectable jewellers would content themselves with *serving* a client.

sleight/slight

There is no such thing as *a slight of hand*. *Sleight* is the word to use in this context: it means 'skill, dexterity, cunning'. *Slight* means 'small, slim' or 'trifling, unimportant' as in *a **slightly** built girl, a **slight** chance of rain, a **slight** mistake*. It also means 'insult', as either a noun or a verb:

> *She was **slighted** by his refusal*
> *His refusal was a **slight** on her character*

stationary/stationery

It is easy to distinguish between these frequently confused words if one remembers that *stationery* (paper, pens and the like) is purchased from a *stationer's*. *Stationary* means 'still, unmoving'.

story/storey

In British English the various levels of a building are *storeys*. The plural of *story*, a fictional account, is *stories*.

straighten/straiten

To straighten is the verb associated with *straight*, meaning 'upright, not bent'. *To straiten* means 'to limit' (it is connected with *strait*, a narrow stretch of water) and is most commonly used to refer to financial restrictions in the expression *straitened circumstances*. *Strait-laced*, meaning narrowly bound by convention or ideas of respectability, and *straitjacket*, were one to have the misfortune to have recourse to one, should also be spelt this way.

their/there/they're

Their is a possessive pronoun meaning 'belonging to them':

> *Gerald and Annabel were unable to settle **their** differences*
> *Once they had looked at the map, they managed to find **their** way home*

There is most commonly an adverb denoting place:

> *I don't think this is the right place for the picture: I would prefer to hang it **there***
> *I was interested to hear about their holiday in Egypt because I had never been **there***

It can also be used, almost meaninglessly, as the grammatical subject of a sentence (see also page 38):

> ***There** is no reason why you shouldn't go*
> ***There** used to be a post office in the village*

They're is short for 'they are':

> ***They're** going to be staying with me, so you will meet them next week*
> *The children are so boisterous that the house seems empty when **they're** not there*

to/too/two

Three of the most common words in the English language, *to, too* and *two* are surprisingly frequently confused and misspelt. *To* is the preposition:

> *You shall go **to*** (indicating destination) *the ball*
> *From dawn **to*** (until) *dusk*
> *A dance **to*** (accompanied by) *the music of time*

and so on. *Too* means also, and is also indicative of excess:

> *If he is going, I want to go **too***
> *There are **too** many people going already*

Two is the number between one and three.

tortuous/torturous

Torturous is connected with *torture; tortuous* means (literally) twisting or (metaphorically) devious. Thus *a **tortuous** route* may mean one that is full of twists and turns; or it may be a cunning way of avoiding a toll road. *A **torturous** route* suggests that the journey caused extreme anguish.

tow/toe

To tow means to pull, as when a boat is drawn by horses walking along a canal *tow path*. *To toe the line* means not to pull it but to put one's *toe* against it, as at the start of a race. Metaphorically, therefore, it means 'to behave according to instructions, to say and do nothing controversial'.

troop/troupe

Like *corps* and *corpse* (see above), these two words have similar origins but have developed separate meanings. A *troupe* almost always refers to actors or performers – one might speak of a *troupe of acrobats*, for example; whereas a *troop* may be a large group of almost anything – children, monkeys, boy scouts, tourists and so forth – often with the implication that there are too many of them and they are somewhat undisciplined. Fighting forces are *troops* and the verb – *the children **trooped** obediently into the classroom when the bell rang* and in the ceremonial context of ***Trooping** the Colour* – is spelt thus.

whet/wet

Whetting has nothing to do with *wetting*. A *whetstone* is a stone used by butlers and others for sharpening carving knives; *to whet* is literally to sharpen in this way. The verb may be used metaphorically in such contexts as *to **whet*** (not *wet*) *one's appetite,* either for food or for an experience to come.

whose/who's

Whose is generally a determiner (see page 24) meaning 'belonging to whom':

> ***Whose*** *boots are these?*
> *The man **whose** boots you borrowed would like them back*

Who's is short for 'who is':

> *I'm not going to borrow boots from someone **who's** going to make a fuss about it*
> ***Who's** there?*

5

PRONUNCIATION

Nothing betrays a lack of Elegance more surely than mispronouncing a word and one of the worst faux pas is 'mispronounciation'. The noun is mispronunciation, *without the middle o. There are other pitfalls, as follows:*

accidentally
… should be pronounced with its full five syllables, not 'accident'ly'.

actually
This has four syllables – '*act*-you-al-lee'. It is not 'acksherly'. See also page 60.

aitch
Used to refer to the letter *h*, this does *not* have an *h* at the beginning. Pronouncing this as *haitch* is one of the worst possible offences against Elegant English. *HD* ('high definition') is *aitch-dee*, despite what one frequently hears to the contrary on television and radio.

aluminium
Please note the number of syllables and order of the consonants – 'al-you-*min*-ee-um'. *Aluminum,* missing out the final *i* and pronounced 'al-*oo*-min-um', is the standard American form, but should be avoided in Britain.

anemone

The consonants of this flower's name ('an-*em*-on-ee') are often confused, causing some patronising mirth at flower shows around the country: *anenome* is wrong.

asterisk

Asterix is a cartoon character. The last syllable of the * sign is pronounced as it is spelt, 'risk'.

buoy/buoyancy

The colourful marker around which yachts race is pronounced 'boy' and its characteristic floating quality is '*boy*-ancy'.

Caribbean

The emphasis is on the third syllable, 'Ca-rib-*ee*-an'. Stressing the second syllable, 'Ca-*rib*-ee-an', marks one out as a watcher of American television or a Johnny Depp fan.

chic

This is pronounced in the French way, 'sheek'. 'Chick' in this context is Inelegant, to say the least.

collector

Three syllables, not 'clector'.

controversy

This one is controversial. The dictionaries prefer the stress on the first syllable – *con*troversy.

debacle

This is a French word and should be pronounced accordingly: 'day-*bahk*-le' (with the 'le' pronounced as in the French word for *the*) is a close approximation. The last two syllables do not rhyme with *tackle*.

draw/drawer

To draw – meaning to produce a work of art or to pull a cart, for example – is one syllable. A person who performs either of these actions may be called *a drawer*. More commonly, *a drawer* is a section of a dressing table or kitchen unit that may be pulled in and out. In either case, it is two syllables with no hint of an *r* in the middle: Her Ladyship tries not to be dogmatic, but has to make an exception here – *drawrer* is both a non-word and hideous.

eighteen/eighty

Speakers of Estuary English often seem to ignore the fact that these words have a *t* in them, pronouncing them something like 'eh-een' and 'eh-ee'. This is deplored by Elegant speakers; 'twenny' for *twenty* is equally to be avoided, as are 'faw-een' and 'faw-ee' for *fourteen* and *forty*, and many other examples of the same phenomenon.

either/neither

'Eye-ther' and 'nye-ther' (as opposed to 'ee-ther' and 'nee-ther') were considered U in the 1950s and are still the preferred pronunciations in most British dictionaries. They are also Her Ladyship's recommendation.

February

This is another word where people often swallow syllables: it should be '*feb*-roo-are-ee'.

fourteen/forty

See *eighteen/eighty*, above.

furore

Three syllables – 'few-*roar*-ee'. The two-syllable American variant *furor* is archaic in British English.

geyser
Whether this is used to mean a jet of hot water discharged
from the earth or a domestic water heater, the first syllable is
pronounced 'guy'. *Geezer* is an old-fashioned slang term for a man,
and is not a word to be used in Her Ladyship's presence.

harass/harassment
… should both have the stress on the first syllable.

itinerary
'Eye-*tin*-er-air-ee' – a carefully enunciated total of five syllables.

kilometre
… should have the stress on the first syllable, as should *kilogramme*.
When used on its own, *kilo* is pronounced 'keel-oh'; as part of a
longer word it is 'kill-oh'.

laboratory
Like *itinerary* (above), this should be given its full five syllables:
'lab-*or*-a-tor-ee'. Swallowing parts of the word to produce
something like 'labr'tree' is profoundly Inelegant.

meander
The word meaning a bend in a river or a leisurely walk is
pronounced 'mee-*and*-er', not 'mee-*rand*-er', as if it were a
character in Shakespeare.

minute
Minute (pronounced '*min*-nit') is the unit of time: *five **minutes** past
five; I shall be with you in a **minute**.* 'My-*newt*' means tiny.

minutiae
… has four syllables, with the stress on the second: 'min-*oosh*-ee-eye'.

minuscule
The error here is most commonly one of spelling, the result of careless pronunciation: it is not *mini-*.

mischievous
Note the position of the second *i*. 'Mis-~~chee~~-vee-us' is wrong.

misled
A surprisingly common cause of confusion in children or in those who see the word written without considering the context, this is the past tense and past participle of *to mislead* and is pronounced *miss-led. Mizzled* is the past tense and past participle of the verb *to mizzle,* used in some parts of the country to mean 'to rain lightly', possibly producing a combination of mist and drizzle.

mural
This has only two syllables ('*mew*-ral'). Introducing a middle syllable produces '*mew*-ree-al', which is a girl's name.

nuclear
This is pronounced '*new*-clee-are'. Not '*new*-cree-lar' or any other random concatenation of the same letters.

of
… has an *f* on the end. Expressions such as *a touch a class* show no class at all. In Scotland *a drop o' whisky* or *a gathering o' the clans* is perfectly acceptable: the objection is not to a regional accent but to slovenliness.

regularly
This is another word that often suffers from having a syllable swallowed, resulting in something like *reg-you-lee*. It should be '*reg*-you-lar-lee'. The same applies to *regulator* (not 'reg'later').

restaurateur
Note the absence of an *n*. Emphasis should be on the final syllable: 'rest-or-a-*ter*'.

secretary
… should clearly have two *r*s in it: it is not 'secetary'.

schedule
In British English, this is pronounced '*shed*-yule', not '*sked*-yull'.

speciality
Note that there is an *i* before the *t*, making this a five-syllable word, 'spess-ee-*al*-it-ee'. The commonly heard '*spesh*-ult-ee' is to be discouraged.

subtle
The *b* is silent, so the word is pronounced 'suttle'.

temporary
Another example of the need to enunciate all the syllables: '*temp*-or-air-ee' rather than '*temp*-ree'.

timbre
This French word, meaning the distinctive tone of a voice or other sound, is pronounced approximately 'tahm-brr'. When using it one should avoid giving the impression that one is about to fell a tree.

twenty
See *eighteen/eighty*, page 125.

unanimous
Pronounced exactly as it is spelled (with the first syllable 'you'), this word requires careful ordering of the consonants: *unaminous* is wrong.

W

If spelling out a word, always give this letter its full value – *double U*.
Professor Ross (see page 10) mentions a non-U pronunciation
dubby-you; nowadays the Inelegant version is something more like
dubba-ya. Dubya may be used as the nickname of a former
American president but should be avoided in any other context.

whatever

This is another example of the ignored *t* (see *eighteen/eighty*, page
125). *Wha'ever* is wrong in any circumstances, and at its worst when
accompanied by a dismissive shrug of the shoulders.

Where and who?

Many English place names and surnames are pronounced in a way that could not be guessed at if one had never seen or heard the words before. The following have all been known to confuse foreign visitors or mark the native speaker as a social climber:

Ascot	Purists maintain that the name of the racecourse is said as if one were holding a knife sideways between one's teeth: 'esc't', with almost no second vowel sound at all. Giving the *o* its full weight will make people of a certain age think one is talking about a water heater.
Beauchamp	*beech*-*am* (particularly important for Beauchamp Place in Knightsbridge, London, home of a number of fashionable restaurants)
Beaulieu	*bew* (to rhyme with 'few') *lee*
Berkeley	*bar*clay
Berwick (-upon-Tweed)	*berrick*
Berkshire	*bark*shire
Beswick	*bezzick*
Carnoustie	car-*noose*-tee
Cholmondeley	*chum*-lee
Dalziel	*dee-ell* (the emphasis varies: both *dee-ell* and *dee-ell* are heard)
Derby (town and race)	*darby*
Dolgellau	dol-*geth*-lie
Dun Laoghaire	the coastal town outside Dublin is usually anglicised to *dun-leery*
Farquhar	*far car*

Glasgow	the second syllable rhymes with *go*, not *cow*
Gloucester	*gloster*
Guildford	*gill-ford*
Hawick	*hoick*
Hertford	*hart-ford*
Islay	important for drinkers of malt whisky, *ile-ah*
Kirkcaldy	*ker-caw-die*
Kirkcudbright	*ker-coo-bree*
Leicester	*lester*
Lerwick (Shetland)	pronounced as it is spelt: *ler-wick*
Llanelli	*thlan-eth-lee*
Llandudno	*thlan-dud-no*
Llangollen	*thlan-goth-len*
Northampton	*north-ampton*, not *north-hampton*
Norwich	*norrich*
Scone	The town in Scotland, home to a stone that for centuries sat under the coronation chair in Westminster Abbey, is pronounced *skoon* (see page 12 for Her Ladyship's views on the foodstuff).
Shrewsbury	locals pronounce the first syllable as if it were a small mammal; in the name of the public school the first syllable rhymes with *show*.
Southampton	as *Northampton*, above
Torquay	*tor-key*
Towcester	*toaster*
Worcester	*wooster*, with the first vowel sound as in *wood*, rather than to rhyme with *rooster*

The names of English counties ending in *-shire* are pronounced
'sh'r', with no discernible vowel sound. Making *shire* rhyme with
fire tells the world the speaker is American. Similarly, the endings
-mouth and *-folk* are not given the weight that they would have as
stand-alone words, so *Bournemouth* is '**born**-muth' and *Suffolk* is
'**suff**-uck'.

In names ending in *-ham* (*Birmingham, Nottingham*), the *h* is not
pronounced and the final syllable is almost swallowed: 'Birming-
um, 'Notting-um'.

Names ending in *-burgh* or *-borough* (*Edinburgh, Peterborough,
Scarborough*) are pronounced 'burra'. Note that *Middlesbrough* has
only one *o* and is pronounced 'Middlesbra'.

The suffix *-combe* (*Ilfracombe, Castle Combe*) is pronounced 'coom'.

6

SPELLING: THE ULTIMATE CHALLENGE

It would be pointless to deny that English spelling is difficult.
No language that can rhyme jerk, dirk, work *and* murk *but not*
fiend *and* friend, *and contains the words* borough, rough,
through *and* ought *has given a thought to the difficulties of those*
trying to learn to write it correctly. It is the price we pay for having
the richest language on Earth, a melting pot into which scraps of all
the other tongues it has ever come across have been tossed willy-nilly.

Although there are rules, they are often complex, burdened
with exceptions and reliant for their application on a thorough
understanding not only of Latin and Greek but also of the paths
that words of Latin and Greek origin followed in order to arrive
at their modern English form. As an alternative to acquiring such
knowledge, Her Ladyship recommends investing perhaps £35 in
a good dictionary and making constant use of it. She particularly
begs readers not to rely on a computer's spell-checker, as it is easy
to type something that appears to be correct but is not in fact the
word intended (see the many examples of 'confusables' in
Chapter 4, page 94).

In the meantime, here are some words that may cause
confusion because some follow one rule and some – for no
apparent reason – follow another, or because they are just plain
difficult to spell.

Difficult spellings

-able/-ible

With this group there are no rules on which any but the most scholarly can safely rely. Becoming familiar with words one is likely to use is the only practical answer:

abominable

(in)accessible

(un)accountable

(un)acceptable

adaptable

admirable

(in)admissible

(in)advisable

(un)allowable

(un)answerable

(in)applicable

appreciable

(in)audible

(un)available

(un)believable

(un)breakable

(un)changeable

(un)comfortable

(in)comparable

(in)compatible

(in)conceivable

(un)consumable

contemptible

(un)convertible

(in)corruptible

(in)credible

debatable

deductible

(in)defensible

(un)deniable

deplorable

despicable

(un)desirable

(in)digestible

(in)discernible

(in)dispensable

disposable

(in)edible

(un)enjoyable

(un)enviable

(in)estimable

(un)excitable

(in)excusable

(in)fallible

(un)fashionable

(un)favourable

(in)flammable

(in)flexible

(un)forgettable

gullible

(dis)honourable　　　　　　　　*preferable*

horrible　　　　　　　　　　　*(im)pregnable*

impeccable　　　　　　　　　　*(un)presentable*

implacable　　　　　　　　　　*(un)profitable*

indelible　　　　　　　　　　　*(un)readable*

indomitable　　　　　　　　　　*(un)reasonable*

inevitable　　　　　　　　　　　*(un)reliable*

inexorable　　　　　　　　　　*(un)remarkable*

irritable　　　　　　　　　　　*(ir)repressible*

(un)justifiable　　　　　　　　*(dis)reputable*

(il)legible　　　　　　　　　　*(ir)resistible*

(un)likeable　　　　　　　　　*(un)respectable*

(un)memorable　　　　　　　　*(ir)retrievable*

miserable　　　　　　　　　　*(ir)reversible*

(un)missable　　　　　　　　　*(in)satiable*

(im)movable　　　　　　　　　*(in)separable*

navigable　　　　　　　　　　*(un)sociable*

negligible　　　　　　　　　　*(in)sufferable*

negotiable　　　　　　　　　　*(un)suitable*

(un)obtainable　　　　　　　　*(un)sustainable*

peaceable　　　　　　　　　　*terrible*

(im)penetrable　　　　　　　　*(un)thinkable*

(im)perceptible　　　　　　　　*(un)touchable*

perishable　　　　　　　　　　*(in)valuable*

personable　　　　　　　　　　*(in)variable*

(im)plausible　　　　　　　　　*venerable*

(im)ponderable　　　　　　　　*veritable*

(im)possible　　　　　　　　　*(in)visible*

(un)predictable

-ant/-ent

Again, in the absence of a thorough knowledge of Latin, checking spelling in a dictionary is always advisable.

ascendant, ascendancy	*excellent, excellence, excellency*
assistant, assistance	*extravagant, extravagance*
belligerent	*inherent*
coherent	*(dis)obedient, (dis)obedience*
(in)consistent, (in)consistency	*omniscient, omniscience*
deficient, deficiency	*resplendent*
(in)dependent, (in)dependence, dependency*	*(in)significant, (in)significance*
(in)different, (in)difference, differential	*sufficient, sufficiency*
	valiant
diligent, diligence	*vengeance*

*Note the difference in meaning between the noun *dependant*, a person who depends on another, and the adjective *dependent* and its allied noun *dependency*, meaning unable to do without something. A *Crown Dependency* such as the Isle of Man is also spelt thus.

e or no e?

When adding a suffix (*-ing, -able, -age* and many more) to a word ending in *e*, it is common to drop the *e*, producing words such as *loving, likable, nightmarish, unmistakable* and *wastage*. Exceptions occur when dropping the *e* might suggest a change in pronunciation or cause confusion.

In words derived from Latin or French[1], the letters *c* and *g* are commonly pronounced as a soft sound (as in *centre* or *gentle*) before an *e* or an *i*, but as a hard sound (as in *count* or *govern*)

[1] It is an almost incredibly sweeping generalisation that simple, single-syllable everyday words derive from Anglo-Saxon or other northern European sources and their more complicated equivalents from French, Latin or Greek.

before an *a, o* or *u*. Thus the adjective meaning 'able to be managed' retains the *e* – *manageable* – to ensure the correct pronunciation. The spelling *managable* would run the risk of being pronounced 'man-a-gable'. The same applies to *(un)changeable, (re)chargeable, damageable, knowledgeable, marriageable, noticeable, orangeade, peaceable, (un)pronounceable* and *serviceable*, and this is by no means an exhaustive list.

Into the category of 'causing confusion' fall words such as *ageing, ageism, mileage* and *saleable*. Although *aging, agism, milage* and *salable* are offered by dictionaries as alternatives or Americanisms, they all look strange at first glance: could *aging* be pronounced 'a-ging' and be connected to *a-going* or *a-gley*? Could 'agg-ism' be something to do with *agitation* or *aggression*? Are 'mill-age' and 'sall-able' in some way linked to *mills* and *salt*? These apparently rule-breaking spellings have been preferred in the interests of clarity.

In words such as *acknowledg(e)ment* and *judg(e)ment*, British English tends to retain the *e*, but dropping it is unlikely to cause offence, as long as it is done consistently. Note also that in a formal context even a British judge or court passes a *judgment*, to distinguish the formal ruling from the judge's personal opinion, which – like anybody else's – would be a *judgement*.

-ize/-ise

Many verbs ending in *-ize* have alternative spellings ending in *-ise*. The former style is always used in American English; in Britain opinions differ as to which is preferable. The *Oxford Manual of Style* insists on *-ize* (as did, perhaps not entirely coincidentally, the late Detective Chief Inspector Morse); *Collins English Dictionary* and *The Chambers Dictionary* prefer *-ize* but give *-ise* as an alternative, without disparaging comment. Yet many British people (Her Ladyship included) have an irrational dislike of *-ize*, and many British publishing houses specify *-ise* in their 'house style'.

In reality, neither *organise* nor *organize, memorise* nor *memorize, realise* nor *realize* will raise many eyebrows in Elegant circles, but, as with *acknowledg(e)ment* and *judg(e)ment* above, it is important to be consistent once a choice has been made.

The *-ize* option derives from Greek and is therefore never used in the following (whose origins are mostly but not exclusively French):

> *advertise, advise, analyse, comprise, compromise, demise, despise, devise, disguise, exercise, franchise, merchandise, supervise, surmise, surprise, televise*

nor in a number of verbs where the last syllable is pronounced *-iss* (*premise, promise*) – or *-ease* (*reprise*).

What is true of these verbs is also true of their derived nouns: thus *organisation* and *organization* are equally acceptable; *advertizement, supervizion* and *televizion* are wrong.

en-, em-, in-, im-?

All of these may mean 'in' or 'into' at the beginning of a verb; *em-* and *im-* are used when the next letter is *b, m* or *p*:

enclose	*entitle*		*embalm*	*impersonate*
encumber	*entrust*		*embarrass*	*impose*
endorse	*indemnify*	but	*emplane*	*impress*
endure	*infiltrate*		*empower*	
engross	*inoculate*		*imbibe*	
engulf	*instil*		*immigrate*	

See also *emigrate/immigrate, enquire/inquire, ensure/insure* on pages 104, 105 and 97.

When forming an adjective, as in the *-able/-ible* lists above, *in-* and *im-* may also mean 'not', and the same rules apply:

inaudible		*immovable*
incredible	but	*impenetrable*
indistinguishable		
intangible		

When the positive adjective begins with *l* or *r*, the negative prefix becomes *il-* or *ir-*:

illegal
illegible
irregular
irreplaceable

There are no 'negative' adjectives beginning *imb-*, but it is worth noting that the opposite of the noun *balance* is *imbalance*.

To double or not to double?

How does one know whether to write *commited* or *committed, developing* or *developping?* The basic rule is that if the infinitive of a verb *ending in a single consonant preceded by a single vowel* is stressed on its last syllable, as in *commit*, the consonant is doubled; if the stress is on an earlier syllable, as in *develop*, the single consonant remains. In single-syllable words and in compounds of them, the consonant is also doubled (*fit, fitting, fitter; wrap, wrapping; outfit, outfitting, outfitter*).

While this rule may be applied to most verb forms ending in
-ed and *-ing*, care should be taken with nouns and adjectives
derived from them.

> *bigot, bigoted, bigotry*
> *cater, catering, caterer*
> *commit, committing, committee* but *commitment*
> *confer, conferring* but *conference*
> *defer, deferring, deferential*
> *develop, developing, development*
> *envelop* (verb), *enveloping*
> *focus, focusing*
> *gossip, gossiping, gossipy*
> *inherit, inheriting, inheritance*
> *interpret, interpreting, interpreter*
> *occur, occurring, occurrence*
> *prefer, preferring* but *preferable, preference*
> *rebut, rebutting, rebuttal*
> *refer, referring, reference* but *referral*
> *worship, worshipping, worshipper*

In addition, verbs ending in *-l* double the consonant wherever
the stress falls:

> *enthral, enthralling* but *enthralment*
> *fulfil, fulfilling* but *fulfilment*
> *label, labelling*
> *libel, libelling*
> *model, modelling*
> *repel, repelling, repellent*
> *tranquil, tranquillity, tranquilliser*
> *travel, travelling, traveller*
> *unravel, unravelling*

If the infinitive ends in a consonant preceded by two vowels, or in two consonants, the last letter is not doubled:

> *beat, beating, beater*
> *groan, groaning*
> *loot, looting, looter*
>
> *act, acting, actor*
> *appoint, appointing, appointment*
> *desert, deserting, deserter*

For the purposes of this rule, the *u* after a *q* does not count as a separate vowel:

> *quit, quitting, quitter*
> *quiz, quizzing*

Verbs ending in *c* may have a *k* introduced to ensure correct pronunciation of the inflected forms:

> *mimic* but *mimicking*
> *picnic* but *picnicking, picnicker*
> *traffic* but *trafficking, trafficker*

-our

American spelling is rendered more straightforward by the omission of the silent *u* in such words as *colour* and *favour*. The British have to take more pains over the compounds of these words:

> *armour, armoury*
> *behaviour, behavioural*

colour, colourful but *coloration*
enamour, enamoured, paramour but *amorous*
favour, favourite, favouritism
flavour, flavourful, flavourless, flavoursome
glamour but *glamorous, glamorise*
(dis)honour, (dis)honourable but *honorarium, honorary*
humour but *humorous*
labour but *laborious*
neighbour, neighbourhood, neighbourly
odour but *odorous* (also *malodorous*)
rancour but *rancorous*
rigour but *rigorous*
valour but *valorous*
vapour but *vaporise*
vigour but *vigorous*

Note that it is both courteous and correct to use the American spelling (without the *u*) when referring to places or works that originate in that part of the world: thus *Pearl Harbor* and *The Color of Money*.

s or c?

Advice is the noun, *advise* the verb, so one *advises* someone by giving them *advice*. Because these two words are pronounced differently, remembering this is also a useful way of distinguishing between *practice* and *practise* or *licence* and *license*: in these cases, although both words in each pairing sound alike, the noun is spelt with a *c*, the verb with an *s*. By the same token, *prophecy* (the last syllable pronounced 'see') is the noun, *prophesy* ('sigh') the verb: *I **prophesy** that this **prophecy** will come true*. And by another of the same tokens, the nouns *defence* and *offence* are never spelt *defense* or *offense* in British English.

i before e except after c?

In Her Ladyship's view, this is one of the least useful of
memory aids, because it has so many exceptions. It comes
into its own only when the *-ie* or *-ei* sound is pronounced 'ee':

> *conceive*
> *deceive*
> *perceive*
> *receive*

but

> *achieve, achievement*
> *aggrieve*
> *(dis)believe* (and therefore *(dis)belief*, despite the change
>   in pronunciation)
> *besiege*
> *grieve, grievance*
> *hygiene, hygienic*
> *niece*
> *piece*
> *reprieve*
> *retrieve, retrieval*
> *siege*
> *shriek*
> *wield*
> *yield*

Caffeine, protein and *seize* are notable exceptions to even this
restricted form of the rule.

Ligatures

A ligature was originally two letters that medieval monks ran together to save time when copying manuscripts and that were later cast on one block of 'hot-metal' type. The vowel combinations *ae* and *oe* – often inaccurately called diphthongs – are the ones that concern Her Ladyship here. The modern British tendency is to simplify these spellings, so that what were originally two vowels become one; the exception is in scientific and medical words, where both vowels are retained. (Her Ladyship notes, with an air of resignation, that completely the opposite is the norm in the United States, where *encyclopaedia* and *estrogen* prevail.) Here is a selection of common British words that follow these rules:

amoeba
anaemia, anaemic
anaesthetic
encyclopedia, encyclopedic
foetus
glycaemic (and derivatives such as *hypoglycaemic*)
gynaecology
haemoglobin (and other words beginning *haemo-*,
    connected with blood)
leukaemia
medieval
oenophile (and other *oeno-* words, connected with wine)
oestrogen
primeval

And how do you spell...?

The following is an eclectic, wide-ranging, some might say
random, list of words whose spelling often seems to cause
problems.

abstemious

accommodate, accommodation

acquaintance

allege, allegedly

amok (as in the expression
    to run amok)

archetype, archetypal or
    archetypical

aristocracy, aristocratic
    (similarly
    bureaucracy/bureaucratic,
    democracy/democratic and
    any other words
    concerned with
    government that end
    this way)

artefact

avocado

bachelor

banister (on a staircase; the
    athlete is *Sir Roger
    Bannister*)

beleaguered

beseech

besiege

broccoli

business (meaning a trade,

profession or
commercial activity.
The less frequently
used *busyness* means
'the state of being
busy')

calendar

cannelloni

carcass

caster sugar, castor oil (the
    small wheels on a piano
    are *castors* and the twins
    in the constellation of
    Gemini are *Castor* and
    Pollux)

cemetery

connoisseur

cymbal (the percussion
    instrument)

decipher

definite

delicacy, delicatessen

desiccate

dilapidate(d)

dryer (as a noun – *clothes
    dryer, hair dryer*) but
    drier (meaning *more dry*)

dysfunction, dysfunctional

ecstasy

embarrass

espresso

extrovert

facetious

frieze (the decorative strip
on a wall, as opposed to
freeze, to turn into ice)

grammar

grey (the colour is always
spelt thus in British
English; the tea and the
politician are *Earl Grey;*
otherwise spelling of
the surname is more
commonly but by no
means always *Gray*)

guarantee, guarantor

guerrilla (as in *guerrilla
warfare*)

hangar (for housing
aircraft, but clothes
hanger)

hindrance

hypocrisy

idiosyncrasy (which is *not* to
do with government
– see *aristocracy* above)

introvert

jeweller, jewellery

languor, languorous

lasagne

leeway

ley line

liaise, liaison

linchpin (but *lynch,* to
execute someone
without a trial)

liquorice

macaroni

maintain but *maintenance*

manoeuvre, manoeuvrable

mantelpiece

margarine

margarita

memento

*milligram, millilitre,
millimetre, millipede* (the
prefix meaning 'a
thousandth of' is *milli-,*
not *mili-* or *mille-,* and
the illogical *millipede* –
which should really be
millepede, meaning 'a
thousand feet' – has
evolved to match this
spelling)

misdemeanour

mosquito

moustache

mucus (noun; *mucous* is the
adjective, hence *mucous
membrane*)

necessary, necessitate, necessity

negotiate

nickel (both the metal and the American five-cent coin)

oblige

parallel

paralyse

paraphernalia

pavilion

penicillin

per cent, but *percentage*

persevere, perseverance

phosphorus (noun; *phosphorous* is the adjective meaning 'pertaining to phosphorus')

potato, potatoes

privilege

programme (in all senses except that of computing, where *program* is the norm)

putrefy

quandary

questionnaire

rarefy

repetitive

sacrilege

seize, seizure

separate

sergeant

Siena (the town in Italy); *sienna* (the brownish colour)

skill, skilled but *skilful*

skulduggery

slyly

soliloquy

spaghetti

stiletto

stupefy, stupor

supersede

teetotal, teetotaller

threshold

tomato, tomatoes

vaccinate

vacuum

vinegar but *vinaigrette*

wilful

withhold

yogurt

7

SOCIAL INTERCOURSE

While most modern communication, whether spoken or written, is less formal than it was 50 years ago, there are still people who will be offended by what they see as impertinence, and occasions – such as when writing a job application or a letter of thanks or condolence – when 'getting it right' is important. In the context of letter writing, the late John Morgan wrote in Debrett's New Guide to Etiquette and Modern Manners, *'If in doubt about the familiarity, remember it is always better to err on the side of formality.' This is sound advice that applies in most other social situations too.*

Nancy Mitford strongly objected to being introduced as 'Nancy Mitford'. In literary circles she should have been introduced as 'Miss Nancy Mitford'; her new acquaintance would then have addressed her as 'Miss Mitford' unless invited to do otherwise. In private life she was The Hon. Mrs Peter Rodd and would have expected to be introduced as 'Mrs Peter Rodd' and addressed as 'Mrs Rodd'. Nowadays this formality has largely disappeared and members of almost any peer group address each other by their given names from the first. Introducing someone as 'Imogen Appleby' is therefore perfectly acceptable, unless she is appreciably older than the other person. In that case 'Mrs Imogen Appleby' or 'Lady Appleby' would be preferable, giving her the option of being less formal if she chooses.

Although in Miss Mitford's day a married woman or a widow was always addressed by her husband's given name (Mrs David

Davison) and a divorced woman reverted to her own given name
(Mrs Daisy Davison), old-fashioned 'correct form' now by and large
gives way to the wishes of the woman concerned. It is up to her
whether she is addressed as Mrs, Miss or Ms, whether or not she
takes her husband's surname on marriage and, if so, whether or not
she retains her own surname for business purposes. The courteous
acquaintance will ascertain how she prefers to be addressed, do as
requested and offer no comment, approving or otherwise.

Introductions and greetings

There is only one correct reply to *How do you do?* and that is *How
do you do? How do you do?* is not a question. Her Ladyship frowns
upon the response *I'm very well, thank you* and also on the
alternative greeting, *Pleased to meet you.*

In less formal situations, when someone asks *How are you?*,
the polite answer is *I'm very well thank you, how are you? I'm fine* is
appropriate in casual conversation; *I'm good* is always incorrect
(see page 71). An answer suggesting that one is other than very well
should be given only to family
or close friends who are
genuinely interested in one's
state of health.

*There is only one correct reply
to* **How do you do?** *and that is*
How do you do?

This may also be the place to mention terms of endearment.
These should always be used sparingly and carefully: calling one's
maid *darling* requires the panache of Marlene Dietrich and
addressing casual acquaintances as *darling* is no substitute for having
the courtesy to remember their names. Her Ladyship recommends
that this word be used only to partners, lovers or (one's own)
children. *Dear* and *my dear* are inoffensive provided there is no
suggestion of condescension; *love, honey* and *baby* are not used in
public in Elegant circles.

Forms of address

To quote John Morgan again, '… in all aspects of sophisticated social behaviour, remember that, if in doubt, basic good manners and common sense will always carry the day.' That said, there are correct ways of addressing members of the royal family, peers and other dignitaries, and if one is invited to meet them it is courteous to use the prescribed titles. Knowing that one is unlikely to make a social blunder may also enable one to relax slightly and enjoy the occasion more.

Her Majesty the Queen
Her Majesty the Queen should be addressed as Your Majesty or Ma'am (pronounced 'Mam', not 'Marm').

Princes, princesses and royal dukes and duchesses
All should be addressed in speech as Your Royal Highness or Sir/Ma'am; when written, their titles should be preceded by His or Her Royal Highness. At the time of writing they are:

> The Duke of Edinburgh
> The Prince of Wales and the Duchess of Cornwall
> The Duke and Duchess of Cambridge
> Prince Henry (Harry) of Wales
> The Duke of York
> The Princesses Beatrice and Eugenie of York
> The Earl and Countess of Wessex and their children
>   James, Viscount Severn, and Lady Louise Windsor
> The Princess Royal
> The Duke and Duchess of Gloucester
> The Duke and Duchess of Kent

Prince and Princess Michael of Kent
Princess Alexandra of Kent (the Hon. Lady Ogilvy)

Because royal titles pass through the male line, David, Viscount
Linley, and Lady Sarah Chatto (née Armstrong-Jones), the children
of Her Majesty's late sister, the Princess Margaret, Countess of
Snowdon, do not hold them; nor do Peter and Zara Phillips,
children of the Princess Royal.

Peers, baronets and knights

Non-royal dukes (that is, all dukes except those listed above) should
be addressed as Duke, their wives as Duchess; in writing they are the
Duke and Duchess of X.

The eldest son of a duke normally holds the courtesy title of
Marquess of Y and should be addressed as Lord Y, his wife as Lady Y
(see *marquess/marquis/marquee*, page 112).

The younger son of a duke should be addressed by his given name,
'Lord Sebastian'; his wife is 'Lady Sebastian'. A duke's daughter is
'Lady Eleanor'.

The same hierarchy applies with the children of a marquess, except
that the eldest son's courtesy title is Viscount.

An earl's title is the Earl of X and he is addressed as Lord X; his wife
is the Countess of X, addressed as Lady X. Their eldest son is a
Viscount, addressed as Lord Y, and his wife as Lady Y.

An earl's younger son is addressed in writing as The Hon. James Z,
but in speech as Mr Z. His sister is Lady Clarissa Z, addressed as
Lady Clarissa.

A viscount's children are all 'the Hon.', but addressed in speech as 'Mr' and 'Miss'.

A baron is Lord A, his wife Lady A; their children also are 'the Hon.' in writing but 'Mr' and 'Miss' in speech.

A hereditary peeress in her own right is the Countess of G, addressed as Lady G.

A baronet is Sir Lancelot Lake (addressed as Sir Lancelot), his wife Lady Lake; their children have no titles.

A life peer and his wife are the Lord and the Lady Lake of Camelot, addressed as Lord and Lady Lake; their children are the Hon.

A knight is Sir Charles X, his wife Lady X and their children have no titles.

Members of Parliament, the Law and local government

The Prime Minister, Deputy Prime Minister, Chancellor (of the Exchequer), Lord Privy Seal, Lord Chancellor and Lord Chief Justice should be addressed by their titles, with no name attached. A Cabinet Minister is 'Minister'.

A lord mayor is addressed as My Lord Mayor; if a 'lord' mayor is female, she is known as the Lady Mayor and addressed accordingly. A lord mayor's wife is Lady Mayoress; a lady mayor's husband is addressed simply by his name.

A mayor or alderman is addressed as Mr Mayor or Alderman X.

Religious titles

In the Protestant Church, archbishops, bishops, deans, archdeacons and canons should be addressed by their titles, with no personal name.

In the Roman Catholic Church, the Pope is Your Holiness, a cardinal Your Eminence or Cardinal, an Archbishop Your Grace or Archbishop and a bishop My Lord or Bishop.

The Chief Rabbi is addressed as Chief Rabbi; other rabbis as Rabbi X or Rabbi Y.

On a more personal note

How one addresses one's parents is a private matter. However, when referring to someone else's parents, particularly if one does not know them well, *your mother* or *your father* should always be preferred to *your mum* or *your dad.* For a newsreader to refer to the *mum* of a young murder victim is not only Inelegant but also deeply disrespectful.

In the same vein, referring to one's own relations as *Mummy, Daddy, Gran* and so on in conversation with someone who does not know them is Inelegant; *my mother* etc. is far more dignified, particularly for the first mention:

> *I'm going to visit **my grandmother** next week*
> *I never know what to buy **my father** for his birthday*

Her Ladyship has a Lancashire-born acquaintance who refers to *my mother* even in conversation with her own siblings, as if the woman in question were not their mother too; it is an example from which many people in the south of England could benefit.

Correspondence

As mentioned in the Introduction, Her Ladyship uses both email and text messaging, and is happy to concede that not all the rules that once applied to letter writing are relevant to these new forms. That said, she believes that in formal communications, even electronic ones, certain conventions still apply.

Except in the most casual circumstances, emails should begin with a greeting, just as letters do:

Dear Sir or Madam is appropriate in business correspondence when one does not know the name of the recipient.

Dear Mr (or *Mrs, Ms, Miss,* according to the preference of the woman concerned) *Lewis* is the formal way of addressing someone with whom one is not acquainted, whether in a business or a social context. It is also the most courteous way of addressing an older person. If the woman's preference is not known, use *Ms.*

Dear Amanda Lewis is widely used to address a person one does not know. While only the most old-fashioned now frown on this, it is less formal and less courteous than either of the previous forms: it should be used only in a business context and only if one expects shortly to be on first-name terms with the recipient.

Dear Amanda is used between friends and 'acquaintances', who may be no more than email acquaintances – it is not essential to have met a person face to face before greeting them in this way.

Hello Amanda or *Hi Amanda* is acceptable only when prior email acquaintance is well established. Neither should be used for a first communication.

Letters and formal emails should be signed as follows:

> *Yours faithfully* if the letter began *Dear Sir or Madam*
> *Yours sincerely* if it began *Dear Mr Lewis* or *Dear Amanda Lewis*

In both cases, the signature should be a full name, not merely a given name.

In less formal correspondence, more flexibility is permitted:

> *With best wishes* or
> *Yours*

followed by one's given name will fit most situations; affectionate terms and an X or two after the signature are a matter of personal choice if some level of intimacy has been established.

Although this is not a book on etiquette, it is worth noting that even in this electronic age the old-fashioned letter, card or printed invitation is always more appropriate than an email or text in formal situations (such as an invitation to a wedding or twenty-first birthday party, or a reply to such an invitation), or if what one has to say is delicate or at all likely to be misinterpreted. Handwritten letters or cards are the *only* acceptable way of sending condolences, and the best way of sending thanks for wedding presents or hospitality. Anything intended to convey emotion – whether sorrow, joy or apology – is also better on paper: the sheer simplicity of sending an email makes it easy for the recipient (whose feathers may already be ruffled) to feel slighted.

The body of the letter

Stylistically, letters and emails are subject to the same guidelines as any other form of creative writing. The simplest and most important of these is 'Never use a long word when a shorter one will do.' Using long words puts the author at risk of:

- sounding stilted, awkward, pretentious, insincere or any combination of the four
- using the wrong word or using a word incorrectly.

As Her Ladyship has already remarked, these are the most transparent ways of trying to appear more educated than one is or of trying to disguise humble origins. As such, they can lead only to ridicule and humiliation. Never, ever, speak or write a word without being entirely confident of its meaning, pronunciation and spelling.

Using capital letters to emphasise a point in an email is widely regarded as the electronic equivalent of shouting. Most software allows the use of bold and italic and either of these is to be preferred. 'Emoticons' such as :-) are irredeemably vulgar.

And that, dear Reader, dogmatic though it may sound in what has been intended as a friendly guide, is Her Ladyship's last word.

BIBLIOGRAPHY

Mark Abley *The Prodigal Tongue* (Arrow, 2009)

Bill Bryson *The Penguin Dictionary for Writers and Editors* (Viking, 1991)

Debra Hart May & Regina McAloney *Everyday Letters for Busy People* (Career Press, 2004)

Kevin Jackson *Invisible Forms* (Macmillan, 1999)

Nancy Mitford (ed.) *Noblesse Oblige* (Hamish Hamilton, 1956)

John Morgan *Debrett's New Guide to Etiquette and Modern Manners* (Headline, 1996)

The Oxford Manual of Style (OUP, 2002)

Kay Sayce *What Not to Write* (Words at Work, 2006)

Fritz Spiegl *Contradictionary* (Kyle Cathie, 2003)

Caroline Taggart & J. A. Wines *My Grammar and I (or should that be 'Me'?)* (Michael O'Mara, 2008)

Clive Whichelow & Hugh Murray *It's Not Rocket Science* (Portrait, 2007)

The quotations from Bruce Price's article on Noun Overuse Phenomenon are taken from his website, http://www.improve-education.org/id6.html

Index